Run For Your Life
at 80

Colin Field

Published by Honeybee Books, Dorset
www.honeybeebooks.co.uk

Printed in the UK using paper from sustainable sources

ISBN: 978-1-910616-71-0

CONTENTS

"All the world's a stage,
And all the men and women merely players:
They have their exits and their entrances
And one man in his time plays many parts,
His acts being seven ages."

'As You Like It' by William Shakespeare.

Chapter 1

FAMILY MATTERS

My name, Trevor Colin Field, is of course partly given to me by my parents and part inherited. The so-called Christian names, or names given at christening, are an anomaly in my case, as I was always assured by my parents that I had been baptised but never christened. I showed an independent spirit from an early age, making it clear that I disliked Trevor and had a preference for Colin. My parents bowed to my wishes and henceforth I was, and still am, called Colin. In later years this has to some extent rebounded, in that my association has invariably been with Wales and not with Scotland, for Trevor hails from the Principality whereas Colin was a Scottish hero.

As for my surname, I have reservations about that too! In my boyhood, Sid Field was a successful comedian, but who wants to be remembered after a comedian? Gracie Fields was much surer ground. Gracie, wartime heroine whose wonderfully croaky Rochdale vocal chords immortalised 'Sally' and 'The Greatest Aspidistra in the World' was someone I was proud to be connected with, even if the *Aspidistra* was native to China! At school in South Wales, where the whole school were required to attend Saturday afternoon rugby matches against other schools, my runs down the wing to echoes of 'Come on, Gracie!' bred a love of participating in competitive sport which has lasted a lifetime. The only other celebrity I am aware of who bears my surname is the M.P. Frank Field – like me, with no plural! He is a thoroughly worthy fellow who so often seems to act as the conscience of the Labour Party. He is another who has added some lustre to what is after all a very common word. It means a piece of ground, especially for pasture or tillage - in French '*champs*', in German '*feld*', and what could be more basic than that?

1

My grandfather on my father's side, I never knew, for he died in 1927, nine years before I was born.

William Field was born in 1873 and apprenticed to a tinsmith. He was brought up in Norwich where his father worked as a warehouse man for *Copemans*, a wholesale grocers. The Copemans were Methodist and William chose to become a Methodist Minister and attended college in Manchester for the necessary training. As a Methodist Minister he moved normally every five years, starting his ministry in Sunderland, then moving to Gorleston-on-Sea (where he married), West Hartlepool, Streatham, Cleckheaton (where he stayed nine years) and Bristol (where he stayed only three years) and finally back to Sunderland where he died in 1927. Between 1915 and 1919 he was a chaplain in the army during the First World War. He attained the rank of Major and served in Flanders at Ypres, in France on the Somme, and at Passchendaele, where he was wounded. Then he moved to Italy, Egypt and finally with the army of occupation in Cologne. He was gassed, and received shell shock, was four times mentioned in despatches and awarded the Belgium *Croix de Guerre* with bar from King Albert of the Belgians. He also received the *Order of the British Empire* from King George V at Buckingham Palace in an Investiture held in the Quadrangle of the Palace at 11 a.m. on June 8th, 1920. My grandfather suffered post-war as a result of the gas attack. I wonder if he was one of those at Ypres who went into battle in April 1915 holding wet cloths to their faces hoping this would give some protection against the swirling greenish yellow vapour that was chlorine gas. There were as yet no gas masks for the Allies. He was to die eventually of cancer at the early age of fifty four; to some extent his ill-health could be traced to his experiences in the War.

In 1999 I was staying at Durham and visited Sunderland where my grandfather had his first Ministry at the Franklin Street Chapel from 1892 to 1897 and his final Ministry at the Thornhill United Methodist Church from 1925 to 1927. It was interesting to find in the Church magazine, outlining its history that in that comparatively short period at Thornhill "he had endeared himself to a very large number of people" The memorial service in what had been his church is described as "very impressive". The body of the church and the gallery were packed, and among the pre-eminent mourners and tributes, all his Ministries were represented as well as the British Legion. His remains were laid to rest at Bishopswearmouth Cemetery Sunderland, where I found as a memorial a stone cross about three feet or so high. The metal lettering was somewhat obscured, but by rubbing off some of the dirt it was clearly legible. At the centre top of the cross is inscribed '*Loves Token*' and lower down "*Rev. William Field Major, OBE, CR de G, HCF, Passed to Higher Service August 17 1927 aged 54 years*". I took some photographs and later my father had his parents grave monument cleaned and restored fully. My grandfather was a remarkable man. I wish I had known him.

Below the inscription commemorating him there is another for "*Constance Ethel, Beloved Wife of William Field. Passed to rest April 2, 1972 aged 101 years.*" Now here was someone I knew well. Gran was the organist of the Regent Road Methodist Church in Great Yarmouth. Born in 1871, she was the second daughter of William and Rebecca Creak, a prominent Lowestoft family. She and my grandfather married on 23rd July 1901. Gran outlived her husband by some forty five years, dying aged 101 in 1972. She lived in Mill Hill until she was ninety odd, when her eldest daughter and my mother shared the task of caring for her. This was not easy as she suffered from Alzheimer's disease for the last five years of her life. She fortunately found an interest in doing puzzles endlessly, but lapses of memory caused some amusing situations. On one occasion my father was rather querulously asked who was the strange woman sharing the house; on another, was the portrait on the stairway of the Laughing Cavalier one of our relatives?!

Earlier, Gran had occasionally looked after us whilst my parents enjoyed a skiing vacation. This was quite novel, as one park at Mill Hill had an exciting roundabout, and another had games of cricket, a passion with me. Steam trains also raced through Mill Hill station. Visits with my parents often involved wolfing down her delicious sandwiches in unwritten competition with my brother, whilst our mother looked on until, embarrassed, she felt she had to intervene. As Gran grew older she lost her culinary touch and fried cheese sandwiches became a staple fare, whilst butter became rancid and apples lost their sheen. My father resisted sending her to a nursing home until the old lady was a hundred, though it was mother who bore the brunt of the care required. I gathered that bath night was a particularly difficult duty.

My father also lived until he was ninety five. It was his ambition to live until the Millennium. Once 2000 had been reached, he passed on almost immediately. He schooled at Ashville College in Harrogate. He trained as a research physical chemist and achieved BSc (Hons) and PhD degrees at Bristol University. In his early sepia photos he is pictured with his Douglas motorbike and various girl friends. He spent all his working life with one company, *Standard Telephones & Cables*, which he joined in 1929, aged 24. Perhaps his happiest years were spent in 1929 and 1930 in the company's research laboratories at Hendon. At this time he met my mother and Gwen Goudge was married to Malcolm Field on June 25th 1932 at Goodwin Avenue Church, Mill Hill. Dad worked for many years at STC New Southgate, Woolwich and Enfield before receiving promotion to be manager of their Newport factory with two thousand five hundred employees in 1951. He was extremely conscientious, meticulous indeed, and would often arrive home well into the evening. He retired to Usk in Monmouthshire aged sixty in 1965, where he spent the next thirty five years in happy rural retirement.

Rather like William Cobbett, 19th century author of 'Rural Rides', dad used a bike and a car instead of a horse, to explore his rural environs. He loved the lanes of his adopted county and hated London - Cobbett's 'Great Wen' - and he and mother used to drag me out, somewhat reluctantly at times, for walks in the local woods and lanes. Mother would identify the wild flowers; dad would lead the more pragmatic occupations of mushroom or blackberry harvest. He seemed to revel in finding things to mend, the car to tinker with, or the house to paint or to be rewired. He was constantly on the go, and until his later years seemed to regard relaxing almost as a sin. He had a fund of oft-repeated jokes and aphorisms, some linked to his Durham and Yorkshire upbringing and pronunciation of such words as scōne (scôn) or grăss (grâss). I have written later of his obsession with his twenty five fruit trees in the garden that he designed at Woodford. My brother and I were the beneficiaries of this and a lawn large enough to almost fit in a full length cricket pitch diagonally. We also benefitted from his love of games, especially French Cricket and deck tennis, on the sands in Cornwall or Devon. He was no mean exponent of tennis and badminton and I enjoyed these sports at his Work's clubs as a teenager.

He had his idiosyncrasies. At times when petrol was expensive he would cut the car engine on a down gradient and urge it on by physically rocking in his seat, in order to save gasoline! He would rush from shop to shop in Newport, regardless of other pedestrians, in order to determine the price of the cheapest margarine and make endless lists enumerating how many times this had been done or that used. He hated telephones and American management, and the front doorbell was an interruption. But he loved choc ices, to be braced on a wintry eminence, and his bureau, where he managed all our finances. In so many ways however he was a fine example for me to follow.

My mother was born on January 27th 1910, just five years and five days after my father. She was christened Rosina Gwendoline Goudge, but always known as Gwen. I have photos taken pre-war, showing my cousin Auriol, who is just two months older than me, together in our cradles on the beach at Bracklesham Bay. I have no memories of these pre-war times, but do remember being evacuated to Berryarbor near Ilfracombe in North Devon in 1939 with mother. My baby brother Christopher Rodney was born in April 1940. My father, Dad, came down to see us at weekends and I well remember seeing his car disappearing at the end of the weekend and feeling a sense of loss. Pre-war my mother had been a secretary at *Standard Telephones & Cables*, established in Hendon. After they married, henceforth she devoted the rest of her life to caring for the three men in her life, my father, my brother and I.

Gwen came from a quite different social background to my Dad's. Her mother, my Nan, was the kindest of old ladies. She had separated from her husband, reputedly too fond of the bottle, and came from solid working class stock in the East End. These were cheerful folk whom I was taken to see occasionally, like the matriarchal Aunt Lou (Nan's elder sister), Gladys and her husband Percy and son David and daughter Judith. Also there was Aunt Rose and Uncle Bill (a butcher), Peter and Alan and another Gladys, and their children. In addition were Aunt Lil and her son Keith, and Uncle Tom, a naval man who played the piano, who seemingly had no ties and told good stories. Most of this side of my family had lived in Stratford or Romford and moved out to Billericay or Little Burstead in Essex. One January I renewed what had become a tenuous contact, visiting them on a fiftieth birthday occasion and they made me feel very welcome. Keith, who was about my age, had recently passed on, as had the previous generation; the rest looked better fed to a fault than they were in past days of wartime privation.

Later on in the war, mother, 'Mussolini' and I were again evacuated, this time to my Aunt's 'stately' home on Entry Hill in Bath. I should point out that 'Mussolini' was our name for my brother, whose head was too big for his body and who remained perversely bald. I am pleased to say that this state of affairs did not last beyond the baby stage. School in Bath was Elementary and highly disciplined. This was quite unlike Woodford Green Preparatory School, known as the 'redcap' school, whose denizens were a few grades higher up on the social scale. In Woodford where mother and I lived from 1936 to 1951 she used to threaten me with going to St. Barnabas School which presumably was where those who were destined to fail in life were consigned. It certainly looked more like a prison than a school, and the school in Bath with a railway running behind it was similar. The *Luftwaffe* destroyed the adjacent church to our school one night in Woodford, which caused us to move to Bath for self preservation. I don't remember donning gas masks in Bath!

After the war, life settled down into a delightful childhood. We had what seemed to me an enormous garden landscaped by my father, a large lawn and some twenty five fruit trees planted on the beds beyond the paths surrounding the lawn, and in the more tumble-down area at the bottom of the garden. Here there was a large tree where we had a platform house overlooking neighbours' gardens in one of which was an enormous pylon. Either side of us we had the Ling and Freeman families. The Freemans also had a large and decorative garden. Celia Freeman, the grown up daughter, used to emerge often in her nightgown and call 'Twilly willy winkle, Twilly willy winkle' in shrill falsetto to call her cat in for food. I used to think she must be an operatic diva. Later to my disappointment I learnt she was nothing of the sort, just a trifle eccentric. In time the fruit trees my father had planted grew large and our mother's and his life revolved around picking them, eating the apples, pears, cherries, plums, greengages, gooseberries throughout the summer and bottling the massive surplus. The black Morello cherries always ripened around my birthday on July 14th. Dad used to encase the branches in muslin bags so that the birds could not get at the cher-ries, so the cherry trees looked sepulchral at night time and simply weird by daylight. Mother also made lots of jam. We had fun birth-day parties where apples were tied to strings and our friends and we had to try to eat the 'bobbing apples'. Such long summer days seemed to last forever. Possibly because we were on something called Double Summer time, it never seemed to get dark until between 10 and 11 pm, around our bath time.

Mother's care over our upbringing was unrecognised at the time, but clear to me now. During the War and after, she fed us malt to supplement wartime orange juice. Because I was deemed to have flat feet she made sure I did the exercises prescribed, each day encouraging me. This consideration extended into my youth when I was repeatedly told to put my shoulders back in case I became hunched, for I grew and grew into a spindly six footer. She also encouraged my brother and me into worthy hobbies. In my case, in my teens she encouraged model making, stamp collecting, marquetry, maintaining a scrapbook and later on keeping an allotment. In that scrapbook my almost only press cutting about my mother relates to the South Wales Argos newspaper, where in November 1955 she entered and won a competition for a hand-made Christmas card. This would chime with a talent she had shown at art class at school for illustrating flowers. I still have the most delicately drawn and painted hellebores, signed by Gwen Goudge of the Upper V at Camden School for Girls. Mother had a passion for gardening and tended the garden with loving care. I can see her now with hand fork or trowel in old clothes, gloved, bent over some particular task. She also enjoyed country walks. Later when we moved to Usk, in Monmouthshire, my brother and I were expected to join our parents on long walks lasting an hour or two. It was almost obligatory, but it did give us an appreciation of nature. Later my mother took a special interest in Chris, my brother's work, as a zoologist in Africa and much enjoyed her visit to South and East Africa. At one point she got so familiar with a robin that it would take cheese from our mouths. For some unknown reason this friendly avian was named "Pooch".

Laughingly my mother described herself as 'a sink slave', the lot of many women of her era. She used an old fashioned washing machine with mangle attached. In wartime she queued at *Wheelers*, the butchers, now a smart restaurant in Woodford, to obtain the best she could for us. To overcome egg rationing we had four hens; mine was named Curly. We cowered in the hall waiting to dash to the Anderson shelter next door with her, as dad was away fire-watching from his factory roof. On one memorable occasion we watched a 'doodlebug', its engine having cut out, begin its deadly descent. She grabbed my baby brother and me by the hand and began a run for the shelter. Fortunately we were protected by the bulk of the house, though it blew out windows on one side of 34 Mayfair Gardens, even though the rocket fell a full mile away. She instilled in us good habits like making our own beds, cleaning and polishing our shoes, pressing trousers, covering our books to preserve their appearance and most controversial of all assisting with the tedious process of washing the dishes. Countless discussions between my brother and I would ensue as to whose turn it was to do the washing and who did the wiping. For once the sink slave having cooked the meal could relax. Chicken was a luxury reserved just for Christmas. Bananas and ice-cream only arrived after the War. A quarter of a pound of sweets was the ration per week. Once she caught me stealing some sweets and I realised her kindness was not all encompassing. She was very close to her mother and when Nan left us and went to live in an apartment, Mother used to take us from school after a meal at a café to spend some hours with the old lady. Nan Goudge died aged sixty seven when I was thirteen but she, like my mother, made an indelible impression on my life through the security and love they gave.

Christopher Rodney was born on April 6th, 1940, so he is my younger brother by about three and a half years. From early days he showed an interest in nature and was especially adept at sketching birds. At Monmouth School he found his mentor in the Biology teacher, Mr. Rolls. He was a good all-rounder at sport, as well as at his studies, specialising in Science, which pleased my father who despaired of my obsession with books. Chris was a good back row forward in the rugby team, and went on to captain Monmouth School in a season when the team remained unbeaten. He also became Head Boy when the school was in a difficult phase between headmasters, so that he and the Senior Master, Mr. Hatton, ran the school. He went on to Kings College, Cambridge, and developed his interest in Zoology, obtaining a PhD, after research on hippopotamuses in Uganda, for his thesis. An oar decorated our bedroom as a trophy of his participation in the Kings College boat in the annual

Bumps event, where they managed to succeed in catching and thus bumping the next boat on three successive days.

He was a Queens Scout and attended the World Jamboree at Sutton Coldfield, Birmingham, in the 1950s. I visited him in Uganda in the 1960s and it was clear that he was very much in his element. He had learnt to fly at Kidlington, Oxford, while completing his degree and he took me up for some of his game counts over the Queen Elizabeth Park. It was an exciting life. I well remember his Land Rover being charged by both an enraged buffalo and then a warthog, whilst the African driver remained transfixed. The hippo had to be culled as they were multiplying to the detriment of other species. After being shot their bodies, inflated by gases, were then ready for the scientists to take specimens. Whilst in Uganda we both played rugby for Kilembe, a copper mining settlement close to the park. Chris had played for the Cambridge University Sixty Club, a feeder for the University team, and later played for Uganda, Kenya and Cross Keys in South Wales.

My brother's life has been spent in Africa working for the United Nations and latterly Farm Africa in Kenya. His work has been on camels and their many advantages over cattle and sheep, especially to the nomadic tribespeople of northern Kenya, a population so often ignored in the rush towards modern development.

Today, Chris practises transposing, travelling in his retirement between his camel camp in Nanyuki, Kenya, and his family located in Devon, where his wife, Nasra and daughters Anita and Leila are living. He uses his camels for their milk and meat as well as arranging safaris. School groups and the British Army in Kenya are among those who enjoy such experiences. He is President of the Kenyan Camel Association.

My father's two sisters were Mavis and Elaine, the former senior to my father in years, the latter younger. Auntie Mavis was a friendly, chatty individual whom I got to know early in life when evacuated to Bath in Somerset during the latter part of World War II. She had a way of making one feel at ease and was a very accommodating and sociable hostess when we visited in later years, where she and her husband, my Uncle Eric Cuthbertson-Hill, lived in Rickmansworth, Hertfordshire, and Hindhead, Surrey. In both places they lived in rather imposing houses with an historical whiff of minor landed gentry about them. Uncle Eric worked for the Admiralty, had been posted to Singapore and had to leave Singapore in a hurry when the Japanese invaded. He and his family were on the last ship which left. He returned to the East as Commander of Admiralty stores in British-occupied India during the later years of the War. He had an extensive library and gave the impression that he had read most of the literature therein. He smoked a pipe and it always intrigued me as a little boy that he had a worn patch on his lip where his pipe customarily resided. His conversational allusions were often to a previous era: that of Rudyard Kipling's Indian stories or of Holmes and Watson's adventures in late Victorian London. He was a great admirer of Dickens.

My uncle died in 1984 aged eighty two. My Aunt Mavis lived to the age of ninety seven, dying in 1999. In her later years she lived with my younger cousin Auriol who devoted many years to caring for her mother in Ripley, Surrey. Auriol continues to live there when not abroad in some interesting, probably adventurous or botanical location. Auriol is a similar age to myself and like my father and brother has a PhD degree. Her work was in research in micro-biology during which she attended several interesting committees. Today she is a leading expert on alpines and is probably the most adventurous member of our generation of Fields and Hills having sea dived, para-glided, rock climbed, sky dived, flown gliders and caved. We cousins were probably closer in our youth than today when we are spread across three continents. I well remember the Christmas treats when as children our families met in London for a show on ice at the Stoll Theatre or panto in the West End.

Auriol's sister, Maureen was born in 1934 and to this day corresponds regularly at birthdays and Christmas with news of her family. She and husband Alan Waltho live in retirement on a very pleasant development in Silicon Valley, San José in California. Maureen rubbed shoulders with the famous when Secretary to Winston Churchill's son Randolph for a while. She also worked at the old Denham film studios before setting up home in Christchurch, Hants, and emigrating to Canada in the 1960s where one of her three children was born.

Both sisters still enjoy a healthy lifestyle. Auriol leads walking groups and her leisure is also spent on our inland waterways, canal boating. Maureen is a habitué of her local swimming pool and jacuzzi.

Another Doctor of Philosophy in the Hill/Field/Creak family topography was Elaine Field, my father's younger sister. Elaine trained at Great Ormond Street before embarking on a distinguished medical career in Penang, Singapore and Hong Kong. In both of the latter cities she founded voluntary organisations for child care. In Singapore she worked as Senior Paediatric Specialist from 1955 to 1961 and in Hong Kong she spent nine years expanding the Department of Paediatrics within the University Medical Facility.

Once retired to Grayshott, Surrey in 1971, she showed a passion for painting and later in Bexhill-on-Sea exhibited some creditable works of art, excelling in still life. As an ever-present memory of her I still have some of her paintings on show and in my bookshelves her book entitled 'Growing up in Hong Kong'. It is a study on the development and rearing of Chinese children, the first of its kind in Hong Kong.

My debt to Elaine is considerable and it illustrates her generosity in that she helped me over a difficult period of my life financially. I think she felt in part that this was a repayment for my father's assistance to her, enabling her to take up a medical career. This was her life's work from which so many benefited and continue to benefit, especially in the Far East, to this day. In that sense she lives on.

With my aunts, my father and their mother we came to an end of an era in our Field family. All lived long and full lives. The average at passing of the four of them was no less than ninety six years. Surely, that must be some kind of record!

Chapter 2

EARLY DAYS

As a future teacher of History I had the foresight to be born on Bastille Day, July 14th, 1936. A.J.P. Taylor, in a memorable pronouncement, regards the year 1936 as a watershed in world history. It was the year in which German troops occupied the demilitarised Rhineland, thereby flouting the League of Nations and provoking the French. Hitler knew he was taking an enormous risk, but he got away with it, and Europe blundered into World War Two. Had Hitler's bluff been called in 1936, history would have taken a different path. All of which is a way of saying, maybe I was destined to be born on the fourteenth day of July in the year of 1936.

Woodford Green Preparatory School in Essex, which had a distinctive red blazer and cap as uniform, was my primary school, but by then the first bombs were being dropped, heralding the London Blitz. At first German aircraft attacked military and port facilities, but in alleged retaliation for British attacks on German cities, the bombing became more indiscriminate. I well remember gas mask drill at school and the air raid sirens announcing a raid, mainly at night. Mother and I gathered in the hall before the dash to next door's Anderson shelter. There, the environment was damp, though there was the excitement of standing at the shelter entrance at night to watch the searchlights probing the sky for enemy aircraft, and hearing the thump of the anti-aircraft guns. The 'All Clear' would sound eventually and we would return home. Next day we would collect the shrapnel, metal shards, deposited in our vicinity during the night.

My memories of evacuation to Ilfracombe, North Devon in the first year of the War are those of a child being hoodwinked when swopping postage stamps by the son of the lady we boarded with. I was afraid to resist this older boy, though I knew I was being 'done' by a not very subtle bit of bullying! Then there was the farm and farm animals at Combe Martin which we visited often, and their maid, Vera, on her knees cleaning the farm floor - an early sexual awakening.

A later evacuation in 1944 came as a result of the new Nazi wonder weapons, the V1 Flying Bomb and the V2 Rocket. This took my brother, Chris, and I with Mother to my Uncle Eric and Aunt Mavis's considerable property set in fine grounds, Granville House, on Entry Hill in Bath. My cousins, Maureen and Auriol, Chris and I lived together for the only time in our lives. Auriol developed peritonitis and in those days when diphtheria was a killer, a burst appendix was reckoned to give only a fifty-fifty chance of survival. Auriol's life hung in the balance. Everyone spoke in hushed tones. Illnesses like this and scarlet fever made an indelible impression on a young mind, something like Ebola today. Another rather irritating feature was my propensity for chilblains in winter, which has returned to plague me again fifty years later.

For a year or so I went to school in Bath, which involved quite a walk to school each day. The school backed on to a railway line. Much time was spent in silence, hands clasped on the desk in front of us to atone for class misdemeanours. Nevertheless, memories of Bath are positive in general. Aunt Mavis looked after us very well and indulged my passion for marzipan on my birthday cake to a fault, putting me off it for many years after. We were very fortunate in not being evacuated to possibly unsympathetic strangers. She and Mother did a good job of caring for the four of us, while their husbands were away on war work.

Apart from wartime evacuation, I was at Woodford Green Preparatory from the age of five in 1941 to 1947. It offered a good grounding under the Headmistress, Nora Read, who set the tone for the school. I include a photo of the sixth form - thirty four pupils immaculately uniformed, all smiling, not in an obligatory manner, but as if they were enjoying the occasion. There was a great deal to enjoy from learning the Prehistoric periods, and our maths tables by rote, to weaving a simple woollen mat. It seems, on reflection, to have been a good disciplined start. In the photo I appear a youngster aged eleven with a fringe, protruding ears, sporting a prefect's badge and with the most poorly tied school tie in the whole class! Miss Read stands, a proud example to us all, at the side. On the back of the original photo I have named all the boys, but only the girls who had made an impression on me, one way or another. Looking at the photo now, it brings back happy memories of challenging lessons, school sports day with egg and spoon, sack and running races, as well as kind teachers such as Ms Swinfern, Garbett, Mabbutt, and Read and good relationships with all my fellow pupils.

Keeping a daily diary is a task I gave myself from an early age, but not until I retired at sixty did I manage to maintain one for a full year. Since 1997 I have kept a daily record however, which I find useful when writing this autobiography but also when referring to the likes of past medical and dental appointments, as well as more pleasant areas of life like friendships, gardening and sporting information and holidays.

So, there follows some original snippets from my diary from January to July 1949 giving some insight into that time when I was a child of twelve. In the front of my Letts Schoolboy's Diary I recorded that the bus fare to and from school was 1½d, that I was the possessor of Locker 259, wearing size six shoes and standing fully five feet one and a half inches in height. I was a collector of bus tickets, car numbers, train names, postage stamps and bird's eggs, regrettably. In brief I collected anything collectable!

Drawing, playing football with friends on the open field of Woodford Green and visiting Nanny, my mother's mother, seems to have absorbed my holidays. On Sundays I went to Sunday school for an hour, presided over by elderly kind Mr Stephen or glamorous leggy Miss Garnham, who once took us swimming to the Kingfisher Pool.

A marionette show, 'The Tinder Box', and the Boy's Own Exhibition "up at Westminster" provided diversions. Post-Christmas parties were punctuated by 'The Land of the Christmas Stocking', a film, followed by a jolly good tea after which I was sick! A cycle ride to Ilford got no further than friend Geoff Davies' house, where we played chess, draughts, and Monopoly. This was perhaps just as well, because another ride with Geoff saw me return home, my knees purple with cold, to chastisement from Mother. My father seems to have spent every weekend fitting plugs!

Now at secondary school I had to stay in for 'Taffy' Jenkins, a Welsh teacher who attempted, without much success, to teach me French. A cryptic note on the first day back adds that 'my poison place' had been bandaged for three days. Now, 'I squeezed the poison out'. 'I scored a try in rugger when Johns went ploughing through and passed to me'. I record the other try scorers and final score, though at the time at Bancrofts School, 'rugger' was a temporary enthusiasm. Daddy's forty fourth birthday came. He had four letters, a pair of red slippers, cigarettes (oh dear!), two cards and a stick of shaving soap; not much by present day standards, but 1949 was post-war privation! Five days later came Mummy's birthday which we all celebrated by having 'a topping tea: nuts, cake, biscuits etc'. She acquired toothpaste, handbag, gloves, writing paper, £5 and two boxes of chocolates and a mincer! She seems to have done rather better, but knew her place!

Some signs of the future awaiting me are discernible. I got good marks for a History test, put my name down for Sports Day, under-thirteen Long Jump and High Jump, and seemed obsessed by the runs I had scored in indoor cricket. My favoured reading was the Biggles books by W.E. Johns, featuring the exploits of a pilot and his mates in early aerial warfare. In woodwork I paid 4d for the book end I had made and mention is made of glasses for reading and for use in the 'flicks' or cinema. I was ill invariably after a film, which rather spoilt the occasion. I still have a serviceable toast rack and letter rack made in those Woodwork classes. It was at this time that we got an HMV television. This put us ahead of all our neighbours, and I was at pains to record how Nanny came to see the television for the first time, and Daddy, ever the technical expert, erected the aerial.

On March 8th 1949 I ran a heat of the 220 yards Under 14 and the next day Long Jumped 13 feet 11 inches. This must mark the start of my athletics career and later on Sports Day I came second in the Long Jump with 14 feet 5 inches. In the Easter holidays we went in the car to Southend. I was amazed at "the terrific length" of the pier, about one and a quarter miles. There was an electric train, but we walked to the end and back. This was followed by a trip to Loughton cinema to see Danny Kaye in the 'Secret Life of Walter Mitty'. It was very funny. On Children's Hour TV, 'Muffin the Mule' and a series called 'Rex and Rinty' were all the rage. The price of Gloy paste had risen from 8d to 1/- in a year! At this age I was branching out, accompanying my friend Brian Tarring, still my oldest friend and now my Solicitor, to Selfridges and to see the sights of London. Previously in 1947, we had been to Lords and the Oval cricket grounds, in a wonderful summer, witnessing Denis Compton breaking all records by scoring eighteen centuries for Middlesex. My passion in the summer of '49 remained cricket, though I followed many sports. Autographs of the cricketers and athletes we saw was also part of my passion for these sports. I well remember going to Ashton Playing Fields in Woodford for the official opening of the track in 1947 with Brian, and obtaining the autograph of the sprinter McDonald Bailey. He reached the Olympic final of the 100 metres at Wembley a year later. June Faulds, we both found very glamorous, and we got her autograph also, after the Women's 200 metres. Unfortunately my diary stops abruptly on July 21st 1949. Whether this was because of the death of Nanny, who had been unwell, or the onset of the long holiday in summer I cannot tell. My thirteenth birthday saw me get a pencil box, geometric instruments and lots of sweets. I received 1/- a week during this period as pocket money, 6d from Mother and 6d from Nan. My school timetable shows that I had school on

Saturday mornings. My exam results already show a bias in favour of the Arts subjects. A 220 yards race on March 8th 1949 resulted in me recording a winning time of 32.5, which as I write sixty six years later, I can hardly hope to match again. Oh that we did indeed return to second childhood, physically!

The reader can gather that I had a wonderful childhood with loving parents who always had time for me, and indulged me in my favourite pastimes: cricket, roller skating and my Hornby Double O train set. This latter was set up in the garage and my father would operate its electrical system, whilst my brother and I watched enthralled as the Coronation Class streamlined blue engine pulled its Pullman coaches on one line, and the goods tank engine its wagons on another. There was never a dull moment, as things were always going wrong. We were confined to the static background of the action. This was the railway platforms and petrol stations, scenery, animals etc, where we could do no harm. On the long summer days which sometimes seemed to last until 10 or even 11 pm, the rails were laid around the garden and the display moved outside. I accumulated a fine collection of Dinky toys and used to enjoy racing these on the carpet in the dining room. This carpet was patterned in the form of a racetrack around the outside. The game kept me occupied for hours.

At the end of the War on VE Day my father, normally a rather sober individual, commandeered my little blue bicycle and cycled madly round the street bonfire, lit to celebrate victory. Occasionally at weekends and on holiday he showed this other side of his nature. He loved competitive sport and from him my brother and I inherited something similar. He was in his element playing deck tennis on a court marked out in the sand. He was so athletic that it wasn't until I was in my late teens that I began to beat him. Mother could see how this hurt him, and we played less thereafter. He was a good tennis player and I joined a club in Woodford in my early teens. Dad had then been transferred to become Manager of *Standard Telephones & Cables*, Newport, South Wales. He had for some time been working there and coming home to Woodford, Essex at weekends. Finally my parents decided to move to a property belonging to STC in Cromwell Road, Newport. This meant leaving Bancroft's School where I had been happy, and the tennis club where I had been even happier, as well as our house 'Trencrom'. I remember crying bitterly.

Mother never took to Newport. It involved a vast social change of circumstances. The smell from the nearby glue works, and the old chap who made a habit of hawking up and regularly spitting in the street opposite our house, were typical of the area. My Mother, though from working class origins, aspired to middle class values. She also missed London.

Recently my brother and I returned to 'Trencrom', the house where we were born, and noted that the iron railings removed for the War effort had gone, as had the almond tree in the front garden, though the beech hedge still flourished. We remembered the coalman lugging in hundred weight sacks of coal on his shoulders, protected by sacking. Down the side path he moved to the coal bunker. Then he deposited the coal down a chute and it made a sort of 'wooshing' sound, soon to be joined by further sackfuls. We also noticed that the cherry tree, though a shadow of its former self, still existed on the small triangle of green in front of our house. Dad parked his bull-nosed Morris post-war there, followed a few years later by an Austin 10, registration GNK 72. They were about the only cars in the 1940s in Mayfair Gardens, a street of some fifty houses!

Our journeys down to wondrous holidays in Devon and Cornwall in the Austin were quite an adventure. Because of the distance to be travelled we left at around 4 am, had breakfast around Stonehenge, and arrived at our holiday destination late afternoon. 'I Spy' games helped pass the time, as the car chugged toward its destination along the notorious A30, with places like Honiton and Tavistock without by-passes causing Dad endless frustration and anxiety over loss of time. How things have changed! Recently I attended my son's wedding near Plymouth, just inside Cornwall, the journey taking under five hours by motorway from London.

These school summer holidays post-War from 1945 to 1951, when aged fifteen we moved to South Wales, saw us explore much of the coastline of Devon and Cornwall. Our first holiday after the War was at Minehead, Somerset, appropriately named, for we were only allowed on part of the beach as the rest was being cleared. I also had measles and so was quarantined for part of the time, which was no fun. However, we enjoyed Carwinnick, Paignton, Kennack Sands and Hayle in the following years.

In 1953 our two weeks was spent in North Cornwall, at Trebetherick. This village located between Polzeath and Daymer Bay made a deep impression. I was to return in later married days with our first-born, Jamie, and again with my parents and my family. Hayle Bay was wonderful for juvenile surfing, the guest house just right and the wide expanses of sand at Daymer and Rock had not a rock in sight! The fishing port of Padstow on the Camel estuary was picturesque and Cornish clotted cream teas a real treat. St Enodoc church, half buried by the sand dunes at Rock, was chosen by John Betjeman as his final resting place. He was not the only one to succumb to the sands, waves, wind and general allure of this special corner of Cornwall. Old photos showing ten of us, Hills and Fields, with Nobby, the Hills' golden retriever, posing for a collective 'selfie' on the rocks at Polzeath takes me back to very happy days.

After 1953, we branched out, became more adventurous, sampling Scotland in 1954 and the Norfolk Broads in 1955. Moving to the end of that decade, there were two holidays in Guernsey and one in Pembrokeshire. By this time I was beginning to resent parental controls and long for more freedom and excitement. This pointed me in the direction of Europe.

Meanwhile I had spent term-time at Bancroft's School, a well rated Grammar school in Woodford. It was further afield than the primary school, so I cycled the few miles there on my New Hudson bicycle, bought for £11 immediately after the War. It still resides as a period piece in my garage to this day. My original bicycle, the little blue one used by Dad to celebrate VE Day, was stolen from outside a sweet shop near Woodford station. The shops there included Sainsbury's, where you could see hams and cheeses being sliced to order on marble counters, and a shop which sold the first bananas to be seen since the War.

The traffic today would make it suicidal to send an eleven year old to school on the route which I used. Bancroft's and Chigwell Schools were those in the locality to which parents aspired to send their sons. I found myself in West House as a day pupil, and succeeded in getting into the House hockey team. In rugby I was put in the second row, probably because I was tall and expected to win the ball in the lineout. Not one instruction beyond that did I understand, so I opted for cross country instead of rugby, an odd decision in hindsight. It was agreeable, trailing most of the group around the woods and ponds on the outskirts of Epping Forest, an activity I was not really made for either.

In the classroom I found an interest in the Arts subjects, though by modern standards they were taught in a strange fashion. The Reverend Sainsbury in cassock and 'dog collar' had a particular party piece which involved quizzing him on difficult word meanings from the dictionary. He was found wanting rarely. Mr Kershaw's way of teaching History was to give a chapter to study for homework and then ask for ten brief factual answers in the test next day. I enjoyed this as I have a good memory for dates and facts, but had little sense of chronology, which didn't seem to matter. Joe Mark, our Gym instructor gave us exercises called 'Swedish Drill' each lesson, and once this was done, we played a sort of gym cricket. He supervised this and did all the bowling underarm. One day he announced that he had acquired tickets for the 1948 Wembley Olympics, and did anyone want to go for around £11 each? This was a lot of money at that time, and for some reason unknown, I decided I wouldn't respond to the offer, a decision I have regretted ever since. It wasn't until twenty eight years later in Montreal that I went to the

Olympic Games. One great advantage at Bancroft's was the enormous playing fields on which we were let loose at lunch time for an hour or so to play our own games. The Great Hall was also an impressive area where Sidney Adams, the Headmaster, addressed the school. I remember particularly the moving occasion when one 'Boss' Wheeler, an especially long serving and loyal member of staff, retired. There were quite a few tears shed.

We loved our teachers' quirks and fancies. 'Taffy' Jenkins, a fearsome French master, was one. 'Daddy' Owens, sloppy in dress, who never spotted me 'cribbing' from notes held under the desk. He was a well-loved character. Mr Bellchamber and 'Bruff' Emptage, neither of whom taught me much Maths, the one too liberal, the other too choleric and prone to fits of rage. Then there was Mr Schaerli, who endeavoured to teach us German by awarding kidney beans as an incentive and who ran a Stamp Club where we could swop stamps at lunchtime. I shall forever remember the timetable on the school day I dreaded, Thursday. It read Maths, Physics, French, Geography and German. Of these the only subject I liked was Geography. Punishments, apart from the cane, which could be meted out at Prefect's Court as well as by Masters, consisted of being given a time period to walk round the quadrangle, a large area of grass in the centre of the school. The Master's Common Room was adjacent. The cane I avoided, but spent many hours walking round the quad.

Recently on one of those weekends which occur once in a year, when places of interest, otherwise closed, are open to the public, I visited my old secondary school. I climbed the many steps to the top of the Tower and admired the fine view. Like the Tower, the Chapel and the Library, I have no memories of visiting these in the four years at the school. As a day pupil I was not living at the school and so was never inquisitive enough to wonder what lay behind closed doors. Age brings a certain bravado and ability to handle situations, which I didn't have as a teenager.

Chapter 3

FORMATIVE YEARS

As recounted already, in 1951 we moved to Monmouthshire, which nobody quite knew whether it was part of Wales or England at the time, and my father worked hard to have our county Scholarships transferred from Essex to our new county. My arrival at Monmouth School was something of a culture shock. For the first few days I found it hard to adjust to the Welsh accent of the boys, for it was a boy's school again. Life as a boarder I took to, as it meant living at school rather than the more restrictive regime at home. I soon found I was able to make a lot of good friends, whose companionship and escapades I enjoyed. There was great rivalry between the two boarding houses, School and New House, the latter to which my brother and I were drafted. The New House was in fact, I suppose, somewhat more recent than most of the school, founded by William Jones four hundred years ago. The Headmaster, the Reverend Cecil Cullingford, was in charge of the New House. 'Cull' was a character alright, who lived with his wife 'Ma Cull' in a private part of the New House, to which I only remember ever entering in the company of my father when being interviewed for entry to the school. 'Cull' would sally forth from his 'holy of holies', gown flapping, a diminutive figure, balding, with a slit for a mouth such that he was nicknamed 'the Mekon' after a fearsome character from Outer Space featured in the popular Eagle comic series 'Dan Dare'. At evening house assembly, he would impress on us the privilege and consequent duties incumbent on being a New House man. 'Ma Cull' was rarely seen, but turned out to be a kindly character when called upon to take me for a check-up on a fractured wrist after a rugby accident. She towered over 'Cull' and was frumpy, while he was smart and officious. His office in the school cloisters was at the hub of things, whence he emerged to collar those who had had the misfortune to drop a toffee paper in the selfsame cloisters, and administered three of the best in his office as immediate retribution.

I was fairly fortunate in entering the school at the age of fifteen, rather than as an eleven year old. In this way I avoided the job of 'fagging' for a senior boy which involved all sorts of menial tasks like cleaning his rugby kit, making his tea or coffee etc. I found myself in a dormitory with twenty other boys of similar age, under one of the New House prefects, a rather sadistic character. I suppose the high point of the boarders' week was Friday after school when we received our pocket money, about 5/- (old money) which we then 'blew' in the tuckshop before going to the Hall to watch a movie. The food was not good. It was said that there were weevils in the porridge and the cook's, Miss Hinman's, pasties were so notorious that they became an object of merriment on Expedition Day. This was a day of freedom to wander, provided one wrote an essay about one's experience, to include in our gang a reference as to the way in which one's packed lunch pasty had been disposed of, the more ludicrous the better, e.g. dropping it from a bridge on to a train passing beneath etc. One memorable Expedition Day a close friend, Charlie Laight, and I went by bus from Monmouth to offer our services to the archaeologists excavating the Roman Legionary fortress at Caerleon. In charge of the digs was Dr Nash-Williams, who asked for our names. "Field and Laight", I replied. He then turned to my friend and asked him for his name, for he had written both names down as one! This simply reinforced our view that such people were potty. I'm afraid we weren't probably of much assistance to that Time Team! Back to the subject of the execrable food. Those who received supplemental food parcels from home were often besieged by the hungry. One character, Merrett, whose family owned one of the largest bakeries in Cardiff, disposed of slices of cake to those who fawned on him the most on a regular basis. I'm glad to say, though tempted, I did not succumb.

Another and probably the only other disagreeable side of life at Monmouth was the Combined Cadet Force. Somehow or other I rose to the rank of Corporal and was expected to drill my platoon, having marched them through the town, on the parade ground at Castle House. This worried me stiff as I was never entirely sure on what foot to give the orders to "About Turn!", "Left Turn!", "Right Turn!" etc. More by luck than judgement, nothing ever went seriously wrong. At the annual camp at Castlemartin in Pembrokeshire or Aldershot, I was placed in charge of a tent and for a week; blanco, brasses, correctly folded blankets etc., became top of one's agenda. It was not my idea of fun, and later one part of the allure of teaching was to avoid National Service.

In contrast, all forms of sport were a joy to me, especially rugby and athletics. At Monmouth I played for the first XV two years running on the wing and enjoyed being a celebrity. The whole school was expected to turn out, all 450 souls, on Saturday on Big Side pitch to encourage the first XV. Ex-Welsh captain John Gwilliam in the 1940s and Tony Jarrett in the 1960s, who established a Points record playing against England, were just two of many notable old Monmothians who played for Wales. Bob Norster and current rugby commentator Eddie Butler also spring to mind, whereas some like Tony Jordan played for England. The First XV Fixture list included schools in England and in Wales, though the matches against Llandovery and Christ's College, Brecon were the highlights of the season. Because I boarded, the school became much more a part of me than Bancroft's had been, and rugby football seemed to manifest Monmouth's ethos most of all. You certainly felt this spirit if you played for the school First Team. Playing on the wing, I lacked subtlety, but had speed. Our coach, 'Taffy' Phillips, taught me how to tackle, and from then on I identified with Welsh rugby and the open style of inventive running rugby played by Wales, and the importance the Welsh attached to the game. Though I have no Welsh blood in my family, I always feel Welsh when 'Land of My Fathers' heralds a Welsh rugby International. It was a proud moment when I was awarded my Colours and the chocolate and gold blazer still hangs in my wardrobe, as a memory of those heady days. Later at Birmingham University it was disappointing not to make a XV, though I enjoyed playing for Chancellor's Hall, the Hall of Residence team.

In athletics it turned out that I was more gifted, though my first experience of competition at Monmouth was not especially propitious. Early in 1952 I represented New House in cross country. The team of six runners competed over a testing, hilly course, finishing along the fields bordering the River Wye. We were pitted against three Day Houses and one other Boarding House, namely Town, Hereford, Monmouth and School. We won the trophy, though I finished twenty-eighth and another of our team, twenty-ninth of thirty runners. This was because we had fortunately four excellent runners who all finished high in the order. The ultimate thrill was to go to the cinema, as a special recognition of our victory, that evening. We saw Marilyn Monroe in 'Niagara'; quite unforgettable. At Monmouth School athletics took second place to cricket in the summer term, and only received much notice on school Sports Day. I eventually won the 100 yards, but it was in the long jump that I excelled. I have a national press cutting of July 1955 announcing that I had broken the school long jump record, which had stood since 1882, by a foot, by registering a jump of 20 feet 2 inches.

Though I took to life at boarding school, my Ordinary Level G.C.E. results were patchy. I passed English Language, Scripture Knowledge and British and European History at the first attempt in 1953. Elementary Mathematics followed in 1954 and French in 1955. Maths was essential for University entrance. A combination of the experienced Mr 'Birdy' Ellis and private tuition under the charming wife of another of our Maths teachers, Mr Bowker, finally brought some enlightenment and genuine interest in Maths, and a pass at the third attempt. In French I was such a duffer that I was put in for an easier Board's examination, to get the necessary qualification, together with my Advanced Levels in History, Geography and

English, in 1955. My father despaired of me following in his footsteps, when I entered the Fourth Year Literary rather than Science. This consigned us to study Agriculture rather than Chemistry, Physics and Biology. Under Mr Day known as 'Boozer', maybe owing to his florid complexion, we cultivated potatoes and measured the water table on a plot, part of the school field. Germinating beans in the laboratory were of more interest to him than complex calculations. For my A Levels I had excellent tuition in the form of Mr 'Burt' Lancaster for English, my Housemaster 'Sam' Bucknell for Geography and 'Mad Major' Parry and 'Fluffy' Stevens for European and English History respectively. Sam was a great enthusiast, and through his approach to the Regional Geography of South America, he inspired in me a desire to visit this exciting part of the world. Parry was a Major in the army, but more importantly he made European History live through examining a series of type written notes, which he issued on a regular basis. 'Fluffy' Stevens or B.J. Stevens was distinguished from Mr S.J. Stevens, known as 'Scruffy' Stevens, our Deputy Housemaster. 'Fluffy' encouraged debate, sometimes out of school, at his house across the River Wye from the school, where he held tea parties for favoured students. It was unwise to provoke 'Scruffy' who was a fearsome wielder of the cane. On one occasion, a dormitory feast which had become rather noisy was interrupted by 'Scruffy', who had a point in that food was taboo in the dormitories, and after 'Lights Out' talking was forbidden. All involved were hauled off immediately and felt the strength of his arm. Sam's remedy would be to reason with us at length, though the end result was the same, if milder.

New House boarders slept in four dormitories, with a Senior Prefect in charge of the three more junior dormitories. When one reached a certain age, one moved into the Senior Dorm, which was unsupervised. In addition, as a privilege of age, you shared a study with a Senior Prefect or could use a 6th Form Study. I am ashamed to say that the herd instinct prevailed, and certain unfortunates' lives were made very miserable indeed by the rest of us. A boy who was Chinese, another who flew too easily into rages, and a third cursed with an excess of spots, become the recipients of our cruel sport. The first was expelled, the second committed suicide in later life, only the third survived the constant pressure.

The only female influence was that of Matron, who would look after any who were ill in a private sick bay. Matron was responsible for our general health. She was a forthright character with a broad Northern accent whose constant refrain was, "Have you brushed your teeth?" On alternate Sundays, boarders were allowed home if they lived not too far away from the school. Otherwise Chapel was compulsory, with an hour long service, with little but the lusty singing of the hymns to look forward to. In my final term at Monmouth I left New House and joined Monmouthshire House as a day pupil, my parents having moved from Newport to Usk, halfway between Newport and Monmouth. Chris and I now travelled to school by bus. Having been made a prefect when in New House, I was now demoted to 'optione', a Roman term for one in training to be a prefect. This was a decision I found difficult to understand, but had to accept. On my final day in school assembly, my prefectorial role was restored. School days had been some of the happiest days of my life. Keeping in touch with Monmouth has been encouraged by an active Old Monmothian Society, which hosts reunions of past pupils at the school each year, and also dinners annually in London, Cardiff and Henley on Thames.

The most impressive gathering of past and present pupils took place at St Paul's Cathedral on 19th March 2014 for a Service of Thanksgiving. This commemorated four hundred years since the school was founded by William Jones, who left a bequest of £9000 in his will to found a school and almshouses in Monmouth. Both the pupils of the Boys' and Girls' Schools, not far short of a thousand, were bussed to London for the occasion, in a fleet of thirty-two hired coaches. Staff, parents, former pupils and distinguished guests formed a vast congregation. It seemed a fitting tribute to an institution that had done much to make my formative years rich and purposeful.

In the autumn of 1955 I arrived at the home of Mr and Mrs Mathews in Edgbaston, Birmingham to start a three year Bachelor of Arts Honours Course in General Arts (History, English and Spanish) at Birmingham University. Another student, Bob Spier, and I had the good fortune to be lodged with the Mathews', no distance from Chancellor's Hall, one of the only two Halls of Residence for students. We had breakfast and dinner at the Hall. Mathews was an ex-Mayor of the City and he and his wife were a considerate couple. Carnival Day saw me in pyjamas and a Donald Duck mask on Birmingham's buses and in the traditional Student Carnival parade collecting four tin cans full of coinage for the chosen charity. I seem to have approached my studies and extra-curricular activities rather seriously. At an evening concert by the Birmingham Symphony Orchestra, Dame Myra Hess played a Brahms Piano Concerto to much acclaim, and at the same venue I heard Sir Oswald Mosley. Sitting near the front, his oratory was loud and persuasive and the meeting rowdy. Several hecklers were ejected by 'stewards' using physical force. I was glad to have had the opportunity of hearing him and his racist views which were anti-black rather than anti-Semitic at the time.

Chancellor's Hall had extensive gardens; the Warden P.C. Hordern's brother, Michael Hordern, the actor, could be seen on occasions strolling there, practising his lines. The main University campus at Edgbaston was not used in those days for academic studies by students studying Arts subjects. For this reason I spent much of my time at the Edmund Street campus in the city. Lectures, seminars and tutorials were punctuated by coffee breaks to the accompaniment of Lonnie Donnegan and skiffle, which was all the rage. At Edgbaston I was drawn to the running track for training, the Barker Institute of Fine Arts, once a week, for a course lecture, and the Students Union, to keep up with all that the University had to offer. Often if the weather was good I walked from Hall to the city centre, bussed to the Edgbaston grounds of the University and walked back to Hall. In this way I got a good finger on the pulse of the city and its better-off suburbs. The Queen Elizabeth Hospital at Edgbaston also housed me for a week after an operation for appendicitis. I found myself in a ward for lung conditions. Many had had a lung removed. One elderly patient asked me to give him a shave; the next morning his bed was closed off, for he had passed away in the night, and I realised that I had attended to one of his final needs.

The main recreations I enjoyed were the 'Wayfarers' and athletics. The former were a society who specialised in relaxed trips into the Midlands countryside. In this way I got to know and like many of the areas adjacent to Birmingham. We hiked down beautiful Dovedale in Derbyshire, from Clun over the Long Mynd in Shropshire and on a memorable occasion got lost in the Wyre Forest in Worcestershire during a midnight expedition. My other main diversion was athletics, where I enjoyed representing the University in the 100 and 220 yards. It was a privilege to compete against Peter Radford and Robbie Brightwell, established stars at the time. I was proud to come second to a Loughborough sprinter in the University's Athletic Union championships in 1959 in the 220 yards. My best ever time was 22.3 in the same year at the University's Bournbrook track. In recognition of these achievements I was awarded an 'Athletics Blue' together with the well-known hammer thrower Howard Payne, for that year of 1959. For fun I decided to enter for Birmingham Walking Club's 'six miles in an hour' event at Kings Heath. I latched onto a race walker who got me through in 59 minutes. It was much harder than I expected and I was relieved to break into a run after the finish.

In school holidays I competed in some handicap events in South Wales. It was exhilarating to win a fountain pen by running a 440 yards, off 32 yards, finishing third at the opening of new playing fields at Caldicot near Chepstow. Our amateur status was not compromised as we received prizes rather than money. Today's aspiring athletes dream of competing in the Diamond League rather than being motivated by clocks and hold-alls picked up at handicap meets!

I cannot say that Birmingham in those days was as full of opportunities as it might have been. The city and the University Union seemed influenced greatly by the Cadburys at Bournville, whose chocolate factory was wonderful, but whose Quaker faith exercised severe constraints. Both city and Student Union seemed to close abruptly at 10 pm. Union Saturday night 'hops', that is dances, certainly did. The outside world intruded sometimes however. Hungarian student refugees arrived after the 1956 Revolt, as did the Soviet leaders B and K, Bulganin and Khrushchev, to be entertained at the City Hall. A wonderful day at Edgbaston saw the West Indian spinners, Ramadhin and Valentine, reduced to ordinary mortal dimensions by Peter May and Colin Cowdrey. Only one wicket, that of Brian Close, fell all day and England amassed a large score. I got thoroughly sunburnt, a small price to pay for witnessing history in the making.

Birmingham in the late 1950s seemed to be in the throes of a construction revolution. The Bull Ring was being revamped, road and building projects proliferated. I wonder if that is reflected in the modern city, for in those days it seemed a pace or two ahead of London in urban renewal.

All good things come to an end; however, I prolonged my time in Birmingham by choosing to complete a fourth year after my degree, for the Certificate in Education. This was essential for a career in teaching, which by this time I had decided to pursue. My motives to be honest were mixed. I wanted to carry on with my interest in History and English Literature, and I did not like the idea of military service, compulsory for two years. Teaching in a state school offered deferment of conscription.

So, after receiving my Bachelor of Arts Honours degree in General Subjects in a ceremony attended by my parents on the afternoon of 5th July 1958, I returned for the Education Year. The teaching practice was spent in a Secondary Modern School in Smethwick and a Secondary Grammar School in the Aston area of Birmingham, whence I emerged a little fortuitously with the Certificate in Education. This is related at length in a later chapter dealing with my teaching career.

In my spare time at the University I enjoyed the Alexandra Theatre and on one occasion went to the Birmingham Variety Theatre which was on its last legs. Numbers flashed up indicating the acts and the whole spirited show ended with the acts throwing oranges and bananas to the audience. This capped a two-hour frolic full of sexual innuendo. I was glad to experience the atmosphere as my mother had always reminisced fondly of times spent at the Hippodrome in Golders Green in North London.

Finally I would say that the men who had done National Service got more from university than we who came to it direct from school. Their extra maturity was evident and they benefitted more accordingly. My relative naivety at the time of the Suez debate in 1956 over the morality of Anglo-French intervention saw me astonished that the Student Union voted against going to war over Suez. Up to then I had led a sheltered conformist existence. It was now time to face the harsher realities of the world outside. I was twenty five years old.

Chapter 4

CYCLING AND EARLY TRAVELS IN EUROPE

Having just read the autobiography of Chris Froome, winner of the hundredth Tour de France in 2013, it struck me that cycling has played a significant part in my life. It has burgeoned as a pastime and a sport in recent years in this country. In some parts of the world it has been part of the way of life to a greater extent in the past.

Travelling in China two decades ago, cars were few, but life on the streets throbbed with open air cycle repair 'businesses' on street corners. Thoroughfares full of purposeful cyclists streaming off to work was very much part of traditional China. In Denmark middle aged matrons use excellent cycle ways to propel themselves into town for the weekly shop. Their 'sit up and beg' cycles have large wicker baskets attached in which to convey the groceries. Holland, like Denmark is flat, so cycling is not too arduous. In France I was struck by the respect which the French motorist has always given to the cyclist, a habit which we seem to have adopted more recently. Maybe it has taken recent British success in the Olympic Velodrome and the Tour de France to bring to widening public notice the value of cycling.

Most children progress from scooter to cycle early in life as they develop a sense of balance and become more adventurous. My first bicycle was a rather striking little blue 'job', bisexual in that it had no cross bar. I treasured it, as my life at the time revolved around it. I couldn't have been much more than 'knee high to a grasshopper' when it was stolen as I was busy buying sweets inside a shop. It was a rude awakening.

After the Second World War was over in 1945, my parents bought me a 'New Hudson' bicycle with cross bar, and exotic attachments like a separate pump, front light and rear bag. It cost £11 and had no gears. One carried a puncture kit and learnt how to detect and mend punctures, which were a fairly frequent occurrence. On this trusty servant, I spent two holidays riding the then fairly uncluttered roads from youth hostel to youth hostel around the South West of England. A year later and I decided to do the same around Wales, whose hills were more exhausting. I remember a day in Snowdonia cycling sixty miles and climbing Snowdon! I enjoyed the challenge and it was little use limiting the mileage as hostels didn't open until late afternoon.

At most hostels I bought a metallic badge with suitable design which I kept and which marked my progress daily. On my first spin I cycled from home at Usk to Bristol, then on to Marlborough next day, to Cranborne to Swanage to Litton Cheney to Exeter, and then to Martock where, arriving at 2 pm to pass the time until the hostel opened at 5pm, I cycled to Montacute. "I had not been there long", my diary recounts, "when a retired Egypt army *wallah* who knew Mr Jones, Governor of Usk Borstal, was talking to me instead of tending his bowling green. He was followed by a sprightly eighty-one year old who gave no smoking or drinking and an Army pension as the recipe for success. He had fought in the Boer War, but his eyes were very bad. Next I helped pull the roller from the verge of the bowling green, and returned slowly to Martock, picking blackberries". Finally to Cheddar next day to Clevedon and home via Chepstow "where at a cycle shop (cum-everything else) my bicycle was fitted up with a new chain link for 6*d*". Most days I did sixty-odd miles, so my appetite for cream buns, second helpings of fried bread and apples filched from orchards along the way, was enormous. I visited many interesting historical sites and waxed eloquent on Salisbury Cathedral which "man seemed to have created to rival nature". It occupied me for half an hour!

A year later, at twenty one, my tour of the Principality took me from Usk to Llandrindod Wells, Church Stretton, Llangollen, Colwyn Bay, Idwal, Snowdon Ranger, Dolgelley, Llangurig, St Davids, Storey Arms and home. Nowadays, having traced this route out meticulously, I can only marvel at the audacity and sheer will power of my youth.

My first trip abroad had been at the age of fifteen, with various classmates. We were lodged in the village of Ellmau, in Austria. I found myself with three others in a house which I came to dislike as I was made to feel unwelcome by two of the others, so in the end two of us asked to be moved. I suspect it was as much a case of being homesick as bullying. Once away from that house, I enjoyed the rest of our stay. The ski resort of Kitzbühl was impressive and we were thrilled to go into Germany and see Hitler's mountain retreat at Berchtesgarten. Another memory of this first trip abroad was of leaving my pyjamas, under the pillow, behind when we left. This indiscretion was something of which I was reminded repeatedly in time to come by my father, who didn't suffer fools gladly.

My passport photo shows an earnest youth, blazer tightly buttoned, tie awry and with a fringe which mother tried to pin back with something called a 'kirby grip', which later I made worse by plastering the fringe down with Brylcreem.

My first travelling experience alone was at the age of twenty three, when I took the ferry across the Channel to see what Paris had to offer at Easter. I remember feeling uneasy and full of trepidation. Fortunately I met Don on the ferry and we saw Paris together for a week. He was the company I needed to bolster my confidence as he was a rather diffident, colourless character prepared to go along with my suggestions. It was exciting as I was experimenting, and taking photos (in black and white of course) in a foreign city and I was so proud of my fancied expertise that the last photo of forty-six in a small special album is captioned '*The photographer meditating April 1960*'. It shows me seated casually smoking a cigarette below a piece of classical statuary in the Tuileries gardens; what a prig! Anyway, I was impressed by what should have made an impression according to the guidebooks: that is the palaces of Versailles and Fontainbleu, the Eiffel Tower, Louvre, Champs Elysses, Sacre Coeur,

Notre Dame, statues of national heroes and heroines, the Opéra and Les Invalides, and the terribly daring Folies Bergere. One photo showing Parisians playing '*boules*' is naively described as "a version of marbles played by adults". I was to learn rather more about the game on a later visit.

The next European adventure was a youth hostelling cycle trip with my cousin Maureen and her fiancé Michael, from Aachen up the Rhine as far as Heidelburg. My other cousin, Auriol, also came. Maureen, being the eldest, was supposed to keep Auriol and me safe. Unfortunately she became a bit bossy and one day Auriol, Michael and I cycled away from her, leaving poor Maureen to arrive at the youth hostel alone. At one point we became genuinely worried for her and the possible consequences of our selfish action. All was well in the end and we enjoyed the youth hostel at Ehrenbreitstein Castle above Coblenz, with a fine view down to the junction of the River Rhine with its tributary, the River Moselle. The Lorelei rock, Luxembourg, a terraced city, and finally Heidelberg, which I was to visit on a rugby tour later, all made an impression. It was August 1958, and the weather was wonderful. We returned by train to England and they left me at Paddington station too late to catch a train home to Newport, Monmouthshire, South Wales. Rather than try to sleep on the platform, I decided to cycle the hundred and forty six miles home! Cycling through the night and then most of the next day I reached home around early evening. I should add that the bike was my 1945-purchased New Hudson with no gears. I remember that crossing the Cotswolds and the final run to Usk from Chepstow were especially tough. I have photos taken before and after this continental YHA tour in 1958 and I seem to have aged rapidly!

In the following year, having learnt my lesson, I borrowed a racing bike with gears and toured Holland with my brother, Chris, who had his own bike with gears, but rather a heavy article. I have a photo of Chris next to a statue of the boy who saved Holland by putting his finger in the dyke. My brother, who proved a stronger cyclist than I, was not as magnanimous, and insisted on using the lighter bike on alternate days, leaving me cursing far behind, as I had once done with Maureen, until I eventually reached the youth hostel. Another photo of me, boarding a pleasure boat to tour Amsterdam's canals, shows me scowling at the camera, full of the hatred I felt at that moment towards my brother. Fortunately it didn't last.

In 1962 I bought my first car, a little Red Mini DAX 109, and in August four of us set out for Scandinavia in it. On reflection it was a stupid idea to travel abroad only four months after the car had been run in. I was very protective of it, and worried lest something happen to it. We saw a variety of ships: the Vasa in Stockholm and the Viking ship and Kon Tiki in Oslo. The Military Cemetery in Arnhem, in the cornfields above the River Rhine, I found emotional; the battlefield of Waterloo a challenge to follow the stages in the conflict; and the Little Mermaid statue in Copenhagen harbour, captivating. In future I vowed not to do the driving, as it occupies too much of your attention.

There was no looking back after my solo trip to Paris and before long I decided that the French Riviera on the cheap, camping, was for me. With a friend, Roger, we saw the sights of Monte Carlo and imagined ourselves with Mike Hawthorne driving the Grand Prix. Somehow we got into the famous casino and fantasised further in the footsteps of James Bond in 'Casino Royale'. This was not, for me, the end of camping experiences, but it was the end of solo camping. In future I went with a minibus full of campers by road, in expeditions organised by an enterprising teacher at Highgate Wood School - Mel Parfitt. My final memory of the French Riviera was spending most of one night on the waterfront at Nice, killing time until my flight the next day. My organising skills were far from perfect at this stage of my life, and the Riviera to me perversely spells privation. I had had a glimpse of the life of the super-rich in their yachts and lavish motor cruisers, and I aspired to something a little more comfortable for myself in future.

Next year I joined a convivial group of teachers, mostly Welsh, from nearby schools in the London Borough of Haringey, and others who had responded to Mel Parfitt's advert in 'The Observer' newspaper. Mel taught Technical Drawing at Highgate Wood School. Ten of us set off in a large, black, rather funeral-looking mini bus for Turkey. We crossed the Alps by the Brenner Pass which included a multi-laned road bridge, then said to be the highest in Europe. On, by way of the Dolomites, Lake Bled, Belgrade, Sofia, and finally through the Edirne Gate in the city walls of Istanbul. Istanbul in 1965 throbbed with life. Most things involved bargaining. Most things were chaotic! During our stay we exchanged money in alleyways, enjoying the belly dancing and resisted the blandishments of those who wanted us to carry drugs back home. Having done my homework, I gave a history lesson inside the Byzantine mosque of Sante Sophia to our party. We crossed by the ferry carrying cartloads of honeydew melons and donkeys to Asia, visiting the impressive hospital at Scutari. It was there that Florence Nightingale tended the sick and wounded during the Crimean War. When Byron, in spite of a clubfoot, swam the Hellespont, a 19th century 'Hero' in search of his 'Leander', how was he to know that today a 21st century bridge links Europe to Asia? Then an all too-brief visit to the Dardanelles and a monument to the Turkish artillery battery who had resisted twenty-two Allied warships in the Gallipoli campaign. It was a case of David and Goliath, which sounds scarcely credible. Whilst on the Asian side of Turkey, we visited the site of ancient Troy (Ilium) on top of an eminence overlooking the Aegean Sea. Homer's Troy of Helen, Achilles and Agamemnon was deep down in about layer six of the strata apparently. We left Turkey through Macedonia and entered what was then Yugoslavia. Mel decided to go through the mountains north of Albania by way of Pec, a seldom used route. Away from roads used regularly, we found the authentic Montenegrins welcoming, and the mountain scenery beautiful. Then, it was down to the Adriatic and one glistening red-roofed, white painted coastal moment after another, each town a contrast from the former, squeezed between the sea and the steep 'karst' limestone cliffs adjacent to it. The idyllic Sveti Stefan, the pearl of the Dalmatian coast, elegant Dubrovnik, the Roman port of Split, and in the country outside Zadar we were invited to a party. It was one of those rare occasions that live forever in the memory. It seemed as if the whole village turned out to feast us and then in a merry state we picked grapes and drew water at the local well. Afterwards we returned to the large communal table, drinking the local wine, laughing and joking, until the sun set, when Mel drove us remarkably steadily back to the campsite. At Plitvice we were impressed by the many lakes and waterfalls and the turquoise waters. We crossed the Alps by the dramatic Gross Glockner Pass and passed into southern Germany. A final and infinitely depressing stop was made at Dachau. The museum, with its heart-rending photographs of the inmates, the soulless living quarters and chimney, stayed in my mind for some time after. It was a sobering end to a wonderful journey, inscribed in the dust on the back of our vehicle for all to see. The vehicle had stood up to it all, including being burdened inside by all sorts of bric-a-brac including a collection of geological specimens gathered by one of the girls, who incidentally was related to the 60's pop icon Marianne Faithful. It had indeed been an adventure as well as an educational experience.

I had enjoyed this trip so much that I joined Mel again in the summer of 1966 to tour Italy with a view to reaching the island of Sicily. Five of our number were Haringey teachers, together with Olive, an acquaintance of Mel's, and Gilmore Jones, with whom I shared a tent. Again, the party had a distinct Welsh flavour. The vehicle was smaller, a promising white in colour, a Dormobile. We arrived at Chillon on Lake Geneva, after travelling through France, and were about to cross the Alps by the St Bernard Pass when I discovered my passport was missing. I had visions of being left at the Italian frontier. The realisation dawned that it had been left at Chillon when I had been taking photos of the romantic castle featured in one of Byron's poems. Mel turned the vehicle round and my relief was considerable when we found that it had been handed in at the local police station in Chillon. I felt like composing a poem in praise of the honest English couple who had saved my holiday! At the top of the Pass there was the hospital and an imposing statue of St Bernard but no St Bernard dogs with flasks of brandy round their necks. At Carrara we stopped at the marble quarries from which the Romans obtained the raw material for their statues and building. Souvenir miniature statues of Venus in many poses and of Michelangelo's colossal David rather dwarfed a solitary statue of Pope John XXII.

The glories of the Renaissance took us to Pisa and Florence. At Pisa, the great bronze doors of the cathedral designed by Bonanno stand close to the famous *campanile* (bell tower), which began to settle sideways, under the same architect who left it incomplete. It was finished at last, almost two centuries later by Tommaso Pisano in 1350. He decided to let it lean and adjusted the proportions accordingly. My musings on the *campanile*, cathedral and rather ornate baptistry were interrupted rudely. Gil's sense of fun was to scare one witless on the top storey of the Leaning Tower by chasing round it. When I tell you he was a rather hefty rugby prop forward, you may appreciate my sense of vertigo in the circumstance. We arrived in Florence on the afternoon that England won the World Cup and watched the match on TV with some Italians in a bar. The Italians all seemed to support Germany. Anyway, to celebrate the victory, we had a few beers and Gil distinguished himself on a skating rink. To finish off a successful day, he and I decided to visit a night club next to the campsite. Being rather inebriated we tried to enter without paying. The 'bouncers' produced razor blades and we left without arguing. Customs in Italy were different it seemed! I then lost Gil and attempted to get into the campsite, which was closed. I climbed to the top of the iron gate and leapt from it. Unfortunately my foot caught in the top rung and I fell, breaking my fall with my hands. I sustained a fractured wrist which was very painful for the next few days. Gil's fate was worse. He arrived in our tent at dawn having lost all his money. On his way during the night it had fallen from

41

his pocket on the hillside and for the rest of our holiday he lived off soup and bread and little else. The campsite, scene of these events, was situated overlooking Florence, a magnificent sight on the Arno, with the *Ponte Vecchio* and the cathedral capped by the huge dome, raised in 1420 by Filippo Brunelleschi. It was the first dome built in western Europe since classical times. The city is girdled by the crescent of the Apennines, which are always visible. It is indeed, seen from the height of *San Miniato al Monte*, the flower of cities.

Through Perugia and the fortified hill town of Assisi we arrived eventually at Rome and camped amid the pines on the outskirts. We did all the guide book things: the Olympic stadium, St Peters, the Forum, the Victor Emmanuel Monument, the Colosseum, Trevi Fountain, Pantheon and many triumphal arches and columns. The architecture in Rome has a size, panache and display fitting to a city once the hub of a great empire. South we sped on to Sorrento in the Bay of Naples, where to escape the throng on the beach, we hired a row boat and attempted to row to Capri. This proved totally impractical, but we compensated, exhausted on the quayside, with the best fried calamares and white wine ever. A mixture of energy expended, relief at calling off what had been patently absurd, and empathy with our surroundings made this a truly memorable meal. This set us up for Mount Vesuvius and Pompeii on the following day. I'm not sure that a glass of the tears of Christ (*Lacryma Christi*) was the best precursor to a hot and hectic day's sightseeing, for I remember having quite a headache. Despite this, the crater of Vesuvius and the Streets of Pompeii, designed for chariots, made a lasting impression on me. Crossing the Straits of Messina to Sicily we moved down the east coast to the vicinity of Catania from where there was a good view of Mount Etna. We had an idyllic day swimming and recuperating among the rocks of the Cyclops Islands offshore. Next day Mel went off to ascend Etna and returned with tales of it being like looking into the mouth of Hell. Like the rest I took the easy option of another day on the Cyclops and regretted I had not been more enterprising.

Our return along the Adriatic coast of Italy was unremarkable apart from visiting Ravenna, which is a monument to Byzantine culture and to Dante. Also there was a first visit to Venice where the sea's the street and where a quiet side canal is often as potent as St Mark's and the Doge's Palace. I was to return to Southern Italy and Sicily, to Tuscany and the Adriatic coast in later years. Together with Spain I find Italy the most wonderful country in Europe. We shall return, but for now let us leave and recount events on two more Mel-led tours of Eastern Europe which follow in 1967 and 1968.

In 1967 we were bound for Romania and the coastal resort of Mamaia on the Black Sea. Certain scenes remain imprinted on my memory. On the way out we visited the 'Hitler' stadium in Nuremberg where the Nazis held their open air rallies. The 'Boys', for we were now an all male group of seven, gave the 'Heil Hitler' Nazi salute on the podium. I shall ever remember a lonely cyclist so surprised by this demonstration that he fell off his machine in sheer disbelief at the sight, staged strictly for photographic reasons, in post-War Germany. We stayed in Prague and Budapest. Both cities impressed greatly, especially the former's medieval architecture and latter's grandiose parliament and bridges over the Danube. South west of Budapest lies Lake Balaton, something of a tourist resort for East Europeans and Russians behind the Iron Curtain. The lake is very large but rarely has a depth of more than a few feet, so one can walk out to a considerable distance in perfect safety. Later I tried night-time skinny dipping with some East German *fräulein*, but was too worried about finding my clothes again on the bank to really take advantage of the situation. Proceeding across the Great Hungarian Plain and into Romania, rural life seemed fairly primitive with mainly horse-drawn transport, cheerful peasants and geese galore. Crossing the Danube by ferry we arrived in the Black Sea resort of Mamaia. Hotel blocks, white and rectangular one after the other, lined the promenade. This was Ceaucescu's communist paradise for the workers, and at the time everyone seemed happy on the crowded beach and campsite. The weather was ideal and the food extraordinarily cheap. A three course meal with wine cost the Romanian equivalent of around £1. Diversions included beach volleyball, mud baths and a nudist beach with which we became fixated. Mel made friends with an incumbent and was ribbed unmercifully thereafter by the rest of us.

We left regrettably having seen little of the feathered bird life of the Danube delta. Bucharest's monolithic communist architecture seemed impressive visually, but lacking character and soul. Passing by a village harvesting, probably an agricultural collective, we stopped and they stopped, pitchforks poised at the unusual sight. The youngsters gathered round curious to be photographed with the foreigners. Had they ever seen a camera? Bobby Charlton, of recent World Cup fame, momentarily brought us together, but in truth we were not only linguistically, but worlds apart. The European Union has begun to bridge that gap half a century later.

The *Portilade Fier,* or Iron Gates, is the dramatic gorge through which the Danube rushes on its way to the sea through the Carpathian Mountains. However we were now well on the way home with a final stop in Vienna, whose palaces are inevitably sad after an era of royalty. Vienna is capital of a vanished empire. The summer palace of *Schönbrunn,* completed during the reign of Empress Marie Theresa, is the saddest symbol of this kind, followed closely by the Belvedere. The glory of contemporary Vienna is the Great Opera House. Mozart or Johann Strauss performed to a full house gives the Viennese their purest pleasure. Vienna's slogan of 'bend but don't break' served them well during the Russian occupation and today the city has recovered much of its pre-1918 grandeur.

We returned bronzed after the 1967 trip and awaited 1968's summer impatiently. This time seven of us did the Yugoslav coastline passing from one picture postcard sun-drenched beach resort to another. The Adriatic coastline here is the most dramatic in Europe, a favourite with the French. Their Citroens' wreckage alongside the route said much for their drivers' empathy with the scenery, if not their concentration.

Later the same summer, a rugby playing friend suggested a trip to Jersey. One incident stands out for me. One evening I agreed to drive our Volkswagen 'beetle' hire car back to the hotel, as the driver was indisposed. Driving alongside St Ouen's Bay in a drizzle, I braked too late and, faced with oncoming traffic, took the option of running into the back of the car in front. Fortunately nobody was hurt badly, as I was uninsured. The law on the Channel Islands is notoriously severe in such cases. The procedure was that the Prosecutor conducts a series of interviews and then presents the case in court. I remember well how everyone, except the two of us, continued to enjoy the holiday, while I faced possible imprisonment for the only time in my life. I was due back for the beginning of the autumn term at Highgate Wood School. A few days, perhaps a week or two inside, would do my career prospects no good. As it transpired, the Prosecutor was generous towards me in his outline of the incident to the judge. I was banned from driving in the Channel Islands and ordered to pay for the damage to both cars. I had been let off lightly. The defendant in the case before mine was less fortunate. In his case there had been fatalities and he was condemned for manslaughter. It could so easily have been me. It is only when you are faced with the possibility of losing your liberty, that you realise how much you value it.

Spain became our oyster the following year. Again we set out in two cars driving across France with my brother, in addition to the other regulars. Mel's guiding hand on the wheel was missed. Our first campsite in Spain was at Donostia in Basque - San Sebastian to you and me. Walking back one night, somewhat merry, we had a brief confrontation with Franco's notorious police, the *Guardia Civil*. My brother and another friend were accused of laughing at them. Certainly their three-cornered hats could have been a cause of merriment. "*No te rias*" was the command; "don't laugh". I was familiar with their reputation and did not fancy a spell in a Spanish gaol, so sounded a warning, and a nasty situation was avoided.

Later in life San Sebastian became a place of much joy for me, despite this sobering introduction. Similarly Burgos with its magnificent cathedral had further associations some forty years later. Segovia's Roman aqueduct is an amazingly impressive structure which dwarfs the traffic flowing beneath it. The city is famous for its roast suckling pork. We were now in real Spain having ascended the *Sierra Guaderrama* onto the vast plateau known as the Spanish '*meseta*'. It is the heart of Spain where the best bulls are bred, full of field after field of yellow sunflowers in the heat of the Spanish 'inferno'. A visit to Philip II's palace of the Escorial, burial place of the Hapsburg rulers, confirms it as the most powerful country in 16th century Europe. The Escorial is more monastery than palace, of unrelenting late medieval energy, dignity and prestige.

Spain is an historian's delight. Its art gallery in Madrid, the *Prado*, brimful with Velasquez, Goya, Titian, and Bosch, has the finest atmosphere of any in my estimate. From Toledo we headed for Portugal. Two days travelling brought us to Lisbon. The impressive monument to Prince Henry the Navigator significantly holding a model of that ideal ship, the Portuguese *caravel*, is on the waterfront. Also there is an architectural gem in Morisco style, Belem Castle, all elaborately decorated balconies, towers, turrets and coats of arms. At Cintra's Botanical Gardens my brother obviously felt more at home, entertaining us with chimp calls and grunts, much to everyone's amusement. You can't take him anywhere!

We returned to southern Spain and Seville, whose belfry of the *Giralda*, nearly 300 feet high, is the minaret of an ancient mosque converted into a church. The Moorish architecture in the *Alcazar* is so much more elegant than the rather grim gothic of the cathedral, one of the largest in the world. Nearing Granada we saw caves on a hillside where people lived in white washed houses set into the hillside, in marked contrast to the elegance of Granada's Alhambra courtyards, arches on spindly columns, fountains, pools and shady gardens. Our journey took us on to Barcelona and the Pyrenees, of which more later.

A final journey with the Welsh 'Boys' took us again across Europe by Minibus, six of us. A Tower of Skulls in Yugoslavia was a reminder that the Turks were not always generous masters, if rebellion threatened in the Ottoman Empire. The object of the trip was to explore Turkey beyond Istanbul. However, on the *autoput* between Istanbul and Ephesus our driver, Glynne, had an unfortunate accident. A Turkish boy was clipped by our wing mirror, when we were travelling at speed, and had to be conveyed to hospital. Apparently accidents were frequent on this stretch, and things looked ugly when a coach travelling in the opposite direction stopped. A crowd got out and appeared threatening. However the Turkish police arrived and we were interned on the campsite, forbidden to leave. Interviewed next morning fortunately one of us, Keri Davies, spoke French, as the police spoke no English. We stated our case and were allowed to leave, though informed that the boy in hospital could die. It was a sober, though relieved, party who crossed the border into Greece later that day.

Chapter 5

MR. CHIPS
My Teaching Career part 1

My teaching career spanned all of 37 years, from 1959 to 1996. In 1959 I left Birmingham University as a qualified teacher with a Certificate in Education. This, rather like my BA (Hons) had a story behind it. The BA Certificate awarded me an Upper Second whereas my actual result was to be lumped with the majority of History and English students for that year in the Lower Second category. I used to make out that I knew the Vice Chancellor's secretary, hence the mistake, but this tale of mine was spurious and simply a means of bolstering my ego.

Similarly, my Certificate of Education had an element of fortune as it required a successful term of teaching practice as well as other merits. My initial teaching practice at Follett Osler School in Smethwick was a revelation to me. During my week at Secondary Modern school, I observed the teacher taking some thirty boys from deprived backgrounds in all their subject areas. The boys were dressed rough and ready, almost Dickensian, but their loyalty to this remarkable man left a deep impression on me. I then moved on to King Edward School in Aston, a Grammar School, where I was to do the bulk of my teaching practice. There, I came under the wing of Watkyn Thomas who, I learnt later, had captained the Welsh rugby team in the 1930s. Unfortunately I never completed my practice, contracting glandular fever and entering the university sanatorium to rectify my blood corpuscle count in early 1960. This, together with hepatitis, a liver complaint induced by too frequent visits to a Yates Wine Lodge in New Street, meant that I received my Certificate of Teaching competence without completing arguably the most important. part of the year's post-graduate course in education. Was this an oversight on the part of the authorities or did they see in me God's gift to the teaching profession? I rather think it was the former, as my tutor in the education year was quite critical when she sat in on my lessons and recordings of my delivery, pronouncing my voice as lacking tonal subtlety.

Anyway the big wide world of London awaited my entry in summer 1959 and I answered an advertisement for a post at Wembley Grammar School. The interview took place in Croydon and I was offered the post at an inflated salary in excess of the sum offered to teachers in state schools through the Burnham scale. The school in Wembley was a small private school run by the Gregg typewriting business and I had been mistaken in thinking it was a bona fide state grammar school. Towards the end of the first term I received my call-up papers for compulsory military service, which came as a considerable shock, as I had not realised that private school personnel were not immune from conscription.

My experiences in Monmouth School Combined Cadet Force were not happy. I had risen to the position of Corporal and been to several camps at Castlemartin in Pembrokeshire and Aldershot and found the 'bull' and regimentation foreign to my easy-going nature. The thought of two years of simulated attacks, drill, rifle inspection, kit inspection dressed in khaki uniform, blancoed belt, and gaiters with shining black boots, filled me with apprehension. There and then I applied for a post at Wayneflete Secondary Modern School in Esher, Surrey as head of the History Department. I was accepted and moved into 'digs' in nearby Thames Ditton in January 1960. My years at Wayneflete were happy times, from then until July 1963, though I found Surrey suburbia less friendly than my Essex birthplace and Middlesex, north of the River Thames. The staff were a jovial lot and the atmosphere sociable. Having enhanced my status and salary by gaining a graded post, I was happy to diversify and soon found myself teaching subjects as foreign to me as art - we built a splendid Norman Castle - and technical drawing. I also volunteered to draw up the programme for the District Sports at Motspur

Park. This was a real headache and taught me to be careful of what I volunteered for in the future and how much goes into the behind-the scenes organisation of such events.

Living in 'digs' led me from Mrs. Bishop in Thames Ditton to Mrs. Price in Claygate and finally Mrs. Pirnie in West Moseley. Mrs. Price had three children, all boys. Her eldest son, Malcolm, had an open white Jaguar and he and I used to drive up to town to 'clubland' for an evening out. Dutifully I wrote about our escapades in my weekly letter home to my parents. I received a stern warning from my father not to worry my mother to death and that I was disappointing his hopes of me. Had he known that I was also dating one of the senior girls at school, he would have despaired, but my trips in my father's *Austin A40 Devon* to Cobham I thought went unnoticed. She was seventeen and I twenty-three. Was it all so unnatural? Nowadays it might make headlines and little did I know, until later, that quite a few knew about it then!

Finally, I settled with Mrs. Pirnie and her son Graham for my last years at Wayneflete. My girlfriend's parents moved from Cobham to the south coast. Was it to avoid my clutches? Mrs. Pirnie held strong leftish political views and took in people from all over the country on a course in taxation matters at nearby Hinchleywood. I sat with them at breakfast. The only ones whose conversation I found the greatest difficulty in following came from Glasgow. Though I did not have a lot of success when entering my pupils for their School Certificate exams, it was good experience, as was my attempt to introduce rugby. My team lost the three games they played. Once in practice, showing how to tackle, I fractured the collarbone of a fleet-footed skinny individual and was relieved to hear that his parents did not deem me to be irresponsible! Nowadays, doubtless compensation would be expected.

Chapter 6

THE OVAL BALL

Rugby football began at the school of that name when, playing football, William Webb-Ellis took the ball in his hands and ran with it. The year was 1823 and for close on two centuries the game has inspired very contrary opinions. Many a rugby wife or girlfriend will empathise with the American writer Virginia Graham whose view was that "women sit getting colder and colder on a seat getting harder and harder, watching oafs getting muddier and muddier". However, I would commend a rather more positive view of rugby as "first and foremost a state of mind, a spirit", given by the French international, Jean-Pierre Rives.

My first experience of the game was at Bancroft's School where I was placed in the second row, probably because of my height, in hopes I would succeed in the lineout. The games master had not made the whole purpose and object of forward play clear, so it was a negative experience and I opted to run cross-country instead.

Moving to Monmouth School in South Wales was a revelation. As related elsewhere, the school *en masse* were expected to line the touch-line on Saturday mornings throughout the late autumn, winter and early spring to support the 1st XV. In this frenzied atmosphere the players assumed the proportions of heroic giants in my teenage eyes. We worshipped at their altars. They were our gods! I found myself relegated as a 'new bug' to an outer pitch where our game was officiated by my geography master, one Sam Bucknall. I doubt if he knew anything more about the game than the games master at Bancroft's, but he noticed that I could run faster than most and recommended promotion to the pitch next to Big Side, the 'holy of holies' ground, on which the 1st team matches were played. Fairly rapid elevation followed and before long I was participating in the practice matches between 1st and 2nd XVs on Big Side under the rugby coach, 'Taffy' Phillips. Taffy immediately put me on the wing and showed me how to tackle. At the age of 17, I was put in the 1st XV and still remember the apprehension and sheer excitement of travelling to our first game away at Crypt School, Gloucester. We drew it 9 – 9. These were the days when scores were lower as tries were worth 3 points instead of 5. Journeys to London to play in the public schools' 7-a-side' competition, and to our brother Haberdasher's Company School at Elstree, were especially memorable for visits to the London theatre, as well as the rugby. In this way one got some intimation of what rugby touring is like - 'a cross between a medieval crusade and a prep school outing'.

From the hero-worship of Welsh school rugby I was brought rudely down to earth at Birmingham University where I was unable to make the 1st team, but enjoyed thoroughly playing for Chancellor's Hall, my hall of residence. The atmosphere was more relaxed and the reputation of the place that the team represented was less at stake. While at Birmingham I had a trial for Newport RFC, whose exploits at their ground at Rodney Parade I took every opportunity to witness when at home on vacation. They were a fine team with legendary Welsh internationals like Ken Jones, Malcolm Thomas, Bryn Meredith, Onllwyn Brace and Garfield Owen on show, but the darling of the crowd was Roy Burnett who had the knack of making superb breaks from outside half. He only made the Welsh team when the wizard that was Cliff Morgan was sidelined through injury. As a spectator, among many memories three stand out. One was in the early 1960s when John Uzzell dropped a goal enabling Newport to beat the All-Blacks at Rodney Parade. Another was when ex-Monmouth schoolboy Keith Jarrett scored a record 19 points at Cardiff Arms Park against England and finally when the peerless Ken Jones cover tackled the All-Black wing Doug Jardine in that Newport victory over the All-Blacks. Only in later years, after he had helped Newport to win the inaugural Welsh Sevens, was the great man seen smoking a cigarette. So he was human after all!

Moving on to Esher I played mostly for their 2nd team, the Cardinals, with an occasional game for the 1ˢᵗs. Esher ran eleven sides at the time involving hundreds of players. The trophy to the club winning the most games, when Esher's eleven teams clashed with those of Streatham, was a human skull backed by goalposts in the colours of the two clubs. A jolly little memento! In one such game, I played on foolishly after being concussed and after the match could not remember what or where my car was. I was taken to hospital and spent a sobering weekend in purdah, whilst my brain composed itself again. Drinking beer in vast quantities was part of the ethos of the game and after matches away we would visit a number of pubs on the journey home. On one early away trip with practised drinkers to play Aldershot Services, I finished at Esher Clubhouse so worse for wear that I spent the night there, mostly in the toilets. I learnt my lesson and made sure this never happened again.

After some seasons with Esher, Priory Park in Southend became my new rugby playing venue. Their selection policy was very fair. My standard was 1ˢᵗ team but if I went home to South Wales and missed a game I was immediately dropped to the 3ʳᵈ or 2ⁿᵈ team, incongruously called the Priors, before ascending the ladder again.

In 1964, aged 28 and back in London, at a school whose Head was Welsh and with a number of Welshmen and women on the staff, I joined Hornsey Hornets, later to become Haringey Rhinos RFC, and played for them until I was 48. The club had been formed as a breakaway from London Welsh RFC and in their first Saturday fixture most of the team, eleven of the fifteen, were Welsh. At times I was to find myself the only Anglo in the team. I loved their singing in our pub run by Scotsman Alex Weir, who would donate a bottle of whisky when we won. The jug of beer would do its post-match rounds and I would often mix my tot of whiskey with the last of my beer. This had dire results later in the evening and my Sundays were often spent in a stupor. Those evenings, sometimes followed by another match on Sunday, put me off whiskey for life! Regrettably, I never learnt to sing with the rest in Welsh and would but mouth the words to get by.

Touring would involve going down to Merthyr or Bedwas by coach on the day before the International against England and playing a hard game on the Saturday morning. Then if you were one of the minority who had a ticket for the game, a trip to Cardiff Arms Park, followed by singing our party pieces, fraternisation, beer and more singing in their clubhouse. On Sunday, we would return weary and dying to sleep but reminded there was no kipping (sleeping) on tour!

One year, my Haringey club recruited a number of excellent junior All Blacks (New Zealanders), who took their rugby and post-match performance as seriously as the Welsh. On driving back from the game one of them, 'Rats', managed to grab a goose from a pond outside the pub and startled me by strangling the poor bird in the back of my car for his Sunday lunch. Another time, a giant Welsh forward managed to remove all the buttons from a cardigan I was wearing in persuading me, none too gently, that I must throw the ball into the lineout just right for him. Happy days!

On the more serious side, as Fixture Secretary, I attended many meetings to make fixtures for the club's four teams for the next season. It became especially onerous when spending much of my lunch hour on Fridays as a teacher in arranging or rearranging the club fixtures.

Tours abroad to Elbeuf near Rouen in France, to Livry-Gargan, a Parisian suburb twinned with Haringey, and to Heidelberg in Germany were memorable. Elbeuf especially gave us a wonderful time on our first tour of the continent at Easter 1966. Arriving on Good Friday, we were whisked away to a cocktail party, a champagne reception at the town hall, dinner at Elbeuf Rugby HQ and a rugby ball finishing at 5am. There followed sightseeing in Rouen on Sunday, another champagne reception held by the Commandant of the Normandy Fire Brigade, a banquet which went on until 2.30am and a final game on Easter Monday. No wonder perhaps that both games were lost, albeit narrowly.

Finally, I hung up my boots in 1984 and took to marathon running, having lost my place in the 1st team in 1981, aged 45. I remain a Vice President of Haringey RFC and in touch with their development both on and off the field.

In 1963 there was an interesting interlude when I played a few games for Western Province in Uganda, based in the copper mining town of Kilembe. In those days, where there were mines there were Welsh, and sure enough that was so. I found the grounds bone hard and grass burns were the only injuries suffered. My brother and I helped them secure the Uganda Cup that year.

In 1975, my year in Canada also saw me introduce rugby into St Thomas High. It was received enthusiastically and with the help of an Australian, John Jones, we coached boys eager to learn a new skill. The school journal commented that the fifteen chosen would be impatient to get on the field and those who do not will want to get on Field! I had a few games playing for the Montreal Barbarians and found the conversion many players had made from Canadian football meant that they tackled ferociously, but had little notion of how to kick a rugby ball. As in Africa, distances travelled to away games were as far as a hundred miles from Montreal to Ottawa each way. In Canada, the hard tackling eventually put me on crutches with a medial ligament injury, which was not an ideal way to face my first term's teaching there.

Chapter 7

THE FAIR SEX

I had better start at the beginning, which was fairly late in life by modern standards. Boarding school didn't help as we were only allowed into town for a couple of hours each week, being otherwise confined to school premises. A few of my peers nevertheless had stories to tell of assignations with a few girls in town and country who were known to be liberal with their favours! I was left to fantasise, and my fantasies centred around a boy rather than girls. Such were my dreams, but never much more than that. Officially girls were on the banned list, together with smoking and alcohol. Monmouth School for Girls chaperoned its charges, gathered together on walks down by the River Wye in a long line known as a 'crocodile'! It caused a sensation when a dance was arranged between the Girls' school and the Boys' school in our gymnasium. Again there was little fraternisation in public as everyone stood about eying the other side timidly. My final memorable and, on reflection, very foolish act at school, was to join a friend, Bernard Mineur known as 'Dungo', in an escapade in the night involving clambering up drainpipes onto the roof of the Girls' school. 'Dungo' was known and admired in New House among his peers as an organiser of japes and pranks. This was about as close as I got to a girl in bed until my early twenties. Incidentally, before I agreed to this escapade I was assured we would not wake anyone and it would not be dangerous. My friend was right on the first count, but on reflection wholly mistaken on the second.

So it was that I arrived at Birmingham University in 1955 aged nineteen, but feeling awkward and shy in the presence of the opposite sex. I remained immersed in study and sport until toward the end of my four-year Degree and Certificate in Education course.

The Education year was seen as a doddle, so I set out to enjoy it and enjoy it I did, ending in the university sanatorium, as recounted elsewhere, but I also found girls. I have a photo of a Birmingham lass, called Susan, and I at the May Ball in spring 1959. By now I had my own study in the hall of residence, Chancellor's Hall, and my father's *Austin A40 Devon*, so I was equipped to at least imitate *Casanova* or *Don Juan*. I remember one young lady telling me she had caused a road accident outside the Queen Elizabeth Hospital because attention had been focussed on her rather than the traffic. I could well believe it. She must have been a nurse and I knew the QE very well, having spent a week there in autumn. So I have good and bad memories of Birmingham's best known hospital, close to its university.

In 1959, I began my teaching career at Wembley. I was twenty-three and in my only term there, I fell for a pupil, Angela, who it transpired was Jewish. She informed me that she could not go out with a Gentile, so that was the peremptory end of that avenue.

As related elsewhere, I had spent over three years in Esher, Surrey from 1959 to 1963. I frequented the Castle Hotel at Richmond and the Assembly Rooms at Surbiton where dances were good places over lager and lime to meet girls; it was a time of fun but little in the way of long term relationships. At one point I became desperate and had a week away at Butlin's holiday camp, Pwllheli, North Wales without being able to lure anyone to my chalet.

By now I was twenty-seven and moving on to Leigh-on-Sea with my own new car, a little red *Mini 109 DAX*, which kept on getting me in trouble, and by the end of its life hardly a panel remained of the original car. The Kursaal at Southend was the new dance hall where I became an exponent of the slow, smoochy dances, the waltz and the foxtrot. On holiday in the Channel Islands, I got friendly with Edith Andrea, an Austrian girl, and we corresponded for a time. And then in April 1964 I met Birgit, a German girl whose father was employed by Lufthansa, in Majorca. There we were part of a group from various European countries who swam and went around together away from our parents, for I was still going on holiday with them. I remember so well a day when Birgit invited me to tour the island in a chauffeur-driven car. Our stop was at a lovely sandy bay called *Cala San Vicente* where we linked hearts traced in the sand, almost Hollywood style. The chauffeur had an enormous paella lunch with us including plenty of sangria, and I then realised why the Spanish have an obligatory siesta. Later that holiday I remember buying Birgit a pearl necklace. I must have been smitten and we continued corresponding for some time afterward. I wonder where she is now; probably comfortably married to a Lufthansa executive! That day in particular, and the mix of young Europeans at the Albatros Hotel, Illetas, Majorca, was one of the happiest holidays I ever had, and goes some way towards explaining my pro-European views.

On returning from Majorca later that April I met Grace, a pleasant steady Essex girl, and we went out together for some months. Finally, in this year of awakening, I met Maria Dolores, otherwise known as Lolita, a Spanish girl living in Stroud Green, N4, for I had moved on in August to Bishopswood Secondary Modern, later Highgate Wood Comprehensive. Lolita was exotic with a beautiful face and long raven, black hair. She dressed well and had a penchant for horror films. She and her parents hailed from Valencia. I took her home and my father was so surprised at this vision that he caught his hand in the mechanism of his favourite automatic chair in offering a seat. There was more than a little further blood spilt over her in her later life I suspect! She was very persuasive and in December 1964, on our way through Mill Hill, I mentioned my parents were attending an up-market dance held by my father's firm. Uninvited, she insisted we gatecrash the event. On reflection my parents must have been very surprised, but took it very well. Eventually Lolita returned to Spain, which suited her temperament better. For Christmas I bought her Edgar Allan Poe's 'Tales of Mystery and the Imagination.'

At this time I was into rugby playing for Haringey and it was at a rugby club dance that I met Barbara. Barbara was the spring and summer of 1966 and I got to know the Uxbridge Road from Mill Hill via Totteridge very well indeed. Unfortunately, Barbara had a young son, Graham, and though I again took her home to South Wales to meet my parents, I was not sufficiently mature to face that challenge yet.

My cousin Maureen and her husband Alan had moved to Canada from Christchurch, Hampshire where I had visited them. In 1971, now 35, I visited them in Montreal, after a very enjoyable few weeks touring the United States and returning across Canada. Alan took me to his office in downtown and introduced me to his secretary, Denise. She certainly made an impression and later when he asked me whether I would like her to show me the French Canadian side of Montreal I agreed readily. Our relationship flowered and continued through a long distance courtship, each writing a letter a week until we met again in school holidays. In summer 1972, I was introduced to the Lamy family summer hideout on a lake in the Laurentians. In December 1972, Denise visited my parents in Usk and we stayed in the Lamy home on Lakeshore Drive in Montreal. A lively New Years Eve was spent with Scottish friends in York. At Easter 1973 I proposed by the lake on Mont Royale in Montreal, after which we went on a camping holiday in Carolina with Denise's friend Sybil and her boyfriend, Denise's younger brother Jean Louis and his wife Marie Paul.

Chapter 8

HIGHGATE WOOD SCHOOL
My Teaching Career part 2

I now return to those thirty-two years spent happily at Bishop-swood, then Highgate Wood School, between 1964 and my retirement from teaching, aged sixty, in 1996. First let me make it clear that Bishopswood became Highgate Wood in 1967, when the former secondary modern school in the London Borough of Haringey became a comprehensive school by amalgamating with Priory Vale School, so changing its name.

After my experiences at Wembley, Esher and Southend I found an establishment which provided a suitable vocational challenge. It provided equal opportunities for a wide variety of secondary school pupils who differed in ethnic origin as well as social background. Schools in Haringey practised a multi-cultural curriculum, more suited to the racial origins of the pupils. During my thirty-two years as Head of the History Department, as well as pupils of largely British and Caribbean origin, we received influxes of youngsters from Cyprus, both Greek and Turkish, as well as from Asia. Added to this racial mix was an equally interesting and challenging British social blend. Children from often quite intellectual backgrounds in Highgate mixed with working class children from the Tottenham side of the Borough of Haringey. The former's parents were firm believers in comprehensive education and included Arnold Wesker, the playwright's offspring, or Robert Peston, a current celebrity and son of Professor Peston at London School of Economics. From other roots came Laurie Cunningham, a football genius.

Under the guidance of a firm and much respected Head Teacher, Eurof Walters, and a senior staff comprised mainly of Welsh Jones' this was fertile ground for a comprehensive system to flourish.

My own department at first consisted of my more-than-able assistant, Ruby Galili, and John Salisbury. John later developed his own Department of Economics and moved on to greater things including Headships elsewhere, being a very successful teacher and motivator. Ruby and I joined the staff together and were the basis of a thriving department for thirty-two years. Ruby continued to run the department for a year after my retirement and then retired herself. The History Department expanded to include four or even five teachers later. Memorable characters included Dave Akerele, son of a Nigerian chief. On one occasion, Dave caught me unprepared when he invited me to a party to welcome his father to London and rather suddenly expected a speech from me lauding his virtues as a teacher as part of the evening's 'entertainment'. Dave was very popular, as were Barbara Bradley and Fran Higgs, both of whom got engaged and were married to other staff members while at Highgate Wood. The department was very successful, if success be measured in good passes at GCSE and A Levels.

Over the years there were many other activities, always peripheral to my main profession as Head of the History Department. For a substantial part of my early career I also supervised games within the Physical Education Department. This might involve umpiring cricket, refereeing soccer or being responsible for a rugby team. As I was later to do in Canada and had done previously at Wayneflete School, I got together a rather motley bunch of older boys to form a rugby team at Bishopswood Secondary Modern. It is rather surprising that with a preponderance of Welsh on the staff and a Welsh Head with links to London Welsh RFC, this had not been done before. Possibly this was because the school was located in a North London hotbed of soccer, halfway between White Hart Lane and Highbury. Anyway it was hard going, as the participants lacked the discipline necessary to absorb some of the games fundamentals and I had not been schooled on how to approach the task. The result was a hearty, well-intentioned rabble full of testosterone, which found sometimes unfortunate expression during and after the game. A school bus driven by me with minimal control of the bus, or these earthy characters, careering down Muswell Hill after a rare win, was a moment to be cherished and never forgotten. Later, after the school became a comprehensive in 1967, the rugby team became a more manageable affair. We used to meet the team at the school entrance gate, early on Saturday mornings, but despite all my powers of persuasion I was never sure that a full fifteen would turn up. Those twin rivals, sleep and soccer, were often too strong! Umpiring keenly contested school cricket matches could also have created awkward situations, especially if one was as ignorant of the leg before wicket law as I. Fortunately, more knowledgeable games staff at schools we visited were very understanding.

Over the course of time as Head of Department I came to understand what sort of history would chime with, what I will term, the average North London secondary school pupil. My predecessor had taught Commonwealth History to his GCSE class. After a year of this and some very average results, the Head suggested British Social and Economic History might go down rather better. He was right. So, for the next ten years this became a much more acceptable and successful curriculum. This was especially the case when pupils were given a choice between that and Medieval History propounded by my very popular colleague, Ruby Galili.

I only altered this after the year's experience as a Commonwealth exchange teacher in Canada from 1975 to 1976, when I was required to teach 'Modern World History'. This was, and as far as I know, still is the modern trend. On my return to Highgate Wood the curriculum was changed with the approval of George Fisher, Haringey Borough's history advisor and proved equally successful, and in every sense contemporary. The introduction of the National Curriculum by the Thatcher government in the 1980s was desirable in the curriculum, though it did lead to a great deal of often unnecessary bureaucracy, detracting from the prime purpose of teaching good lessons. Speaking only about my own Department, previously it was leading to an unbalanced curriculum where British History was in danger of being neglected in favour of a return to Commonwealth History under another guise. Mr Fisher with the laudable intention of promoting history which appealed to those hitherto marginalised, wanted a more positive approach to Black History and emphasis on Asian, African and Cypriot, from the point of view of the indigenous rather than colonial power. Olaudah Equiano and Mary Seacole emerged from the mists of the past to be put aside William Wilberforce and Florence Nightingale, but the process was getting a bit out of hand. A balance has now hopefully been achieved. Certainly I felt that my experience of teaching in Canada, and ten years later my involvement in the European Teachers' Study Tour to Japan, had helped broaden and mature my attitudes to such initiatives.

During my years at Highgate Wood there were only two Headmasters: Eurof Walters, a Welshman and then Jim Smith, a Scot. The senior staff, consisting of the Deputy Head and Heads of Houses, were also fairly stable and effective, which helped establish the reputation of what developed as a successful comprehensive school. When writing an article for the Sunday Telegraph as its Education Correspondent, Robert Peston once asked me what I thought was the most important ingredient to this success. I answered that I thought it to be "good senior staff". He quoted me in his article headed "I came from a Bog-Standard Comprehensive", using a derogatory phrase used in the Houses of Commons to describe comprehensive education at the time. Robert was proud of his school, much as I had been proud of my education at a grammar/public school. My contribution towards this had also been as Schools Exams Officer for the last twelve years of my career and as Deputy Head of the Arts Faculty. Together with the responsibilities of being a Form Tutor answerable for the physical, social and moral welfare of over twenty pupils, the stress levels began to build up towards the end of my career. Finally I had to retire at the age of fifty-nine/sixty owing to a stress-related depression which arrived quite unexpectedly at the end of the winter term in December 1995. I later learnt that such mental conditions were known as 'the teacher's disease'. So ended my professional paid teaching career which was replaced shortly thereafter by a more relaxed and therapeutic twenty years of voluntary History teaching at Enfield University of the Third Age.

Unless this section of my autobiography be deemed lacking humour, the following incidents may compensate. It was the habit to raise funds for Highgate Wood and for worthy charities by a sponsored walk over a distance of fifteen miles. The initial walk took place along the towpath of the River Lea Navigation Canal from Stanstead Abbotts in Hertfordshire to Tottenham in North London on a Sunday in September 1968. In 1981 the school walk happened to be at a time where I was getting interested in marathon running. I decided to take my three-year-old son, James. After a short distance he had had enough and so I carried him for the rest of the way on my back. I well remember arriving at the 'Old English Gentlemen', a tow-path pub in Enfield, with some miles still to go, feeling utterly spent, knowing I had to shoulder the burden again. I relive the moment every time I drive past that spot to this day.

I suppose you remember most those things which don't go according to plan, one or another's miscalculations. There was the case of the persistently awkward and physically 'weedy' pupil who rose enormously in my estimation after he showed me a photo taken of him bungee jumping from the bridge over the River Zambezi at Victoria Falls.

Other's errors included the Head's attempt, following the then trend in educational thought, to get all the teachers to deliver Social Studies. Since many of us had not been trained in the subject or skills required, in practice it was a dismal failure. Similarly, another *avante garde* experiment involved placing another youthful practitioner in my class to instruct me in the practice of group learning, said to be beneficial to the students. Fred was a likeable person and unearthed an Armenian princess in this rather difficult class, apart from which I remained secretly convinced that having pupil-led discussion groups was a way to chaos. Sometimes initiatives could succeed and certainly collaboration with our go-ahead Information Technology Head of Department, Geoff Preston, bore positive results. Geoff guided the students to enter population statistics obtained from censuses on a Victorian street in the Bruce Grove area of Tottenham. With this information they were able to extract from their computers valuable evidence as to the demography of the area. The study was featured in IT journals, as an example in the early 1990s of what computers could bring to the classroom.

Part of the constant fascination of teaching is that one is not only guiding, but also being guided along new paths. Such was my experience from 1975 to 1976 in Canada. Not only was I to be married in the eventful year that followed, but I was also to benefit professionally from a year spent in a new teaching environment.

At Easter 1974 I continued what had been a weekly exchange of letters ever since my visit the previous Christmas and Easter by getting engaged to Denise Lamy near the skating rink in Mount Royal Park, Montreal. I returned to England buoyed with thoughts of forthcoming marriage. First however, a year's teaching exchange with a Canadian teacher had to be arranged so that I might sample the Canadian way of life, preparatory to possibly spending the rest of my life in that country. Contacts were established with Roman Jarymowitz who taught History at St Thomas High at Dorval, Montreal, not far from where Denise and her mother lived, and where her two brothers, Jean Louis and Jean Pierre, ran a pest control business during the week on Lakeshore Drive from a large house. Roman was a strange character whose addiction to military matters led him to do odds things. On occasions he enjoyed lobbing pretend grenades into classrooms or the staffroom, or climbing along the outside walls to appear unexpectedly in the window of the next classroom. This did not go down well at Highgate Wood where such extrovert behaviour was unique. The staff were fairly evenly divided regarding Roman, some enjoying his wayward behaviour, others finding it unacceptable. The exchange went ahead promoted on my side by the excellent League for the Exchange of Commonwealth teachers, who could not have been more helpful. I gave a verbal promise to return at the end of the exchange school year.

In late July I arrived in Canada and on August 10th was married at Dorval's Catholic church. My parents, my cousin Maureen's family, who lived in Montreal, and two of my teaching colleagues, Charles Holman and Andy Adams, meant that there was some English present in an otherwise French Canadian Catholic ceremony. Prior to the wedding I remember being bitten rather viciously facially by mosquitoes, which didn't help my appearance, painting chairs destined for the garden reception, and preparing a speech in French. I stayed the day before at my cousin Maureen's and well remember the hustle, bustle and state of nervous apprehension I felt on that morning as I examined myself in an unaccustomed 'tux' and bowtie.

The day was fine; I said the right things at the right time during the ceremony. Denise looked ravishing in her wedding dress. I well remember getting into the limousine outside the church with a sigh of relief, covered in confetti. The aftermath wedding reception in the large garden on Lakeshore was a grand occasion, not spoilt by the planes flying low on their regular approach to Dorval international airport. At some stage, probably fortified by champagne, I made my speech in French from the balcony to those assembled below in the garden, which was well received. Maureen's daughter Andrea, then just a toddler, came close to stealing the show as little girls often do at weddings. Denise's boxer dog, Gyp, barked excitedly and all the aunts, uncles, cousins and friends had a great time over which Madame Lamy presided, secure in the assurances I had given to bring up any children we might have as Catholics.

We left for our honeymoon in Jamaica at Montego Bay by Canadian Pacific Air shortly after. I was especially excited I suppose, and to this day it remains a memorable flight with china plates, cups and saucers for the only time in my experience which even Thai Air, with their printed menus and orchids, could not match! In our condominium we were greeted with a hibiscus welcome, somewhat marred by the appearance of a cockroach we nicknamed Harry on the first night. That week we hired a car and saw quite a bit of the island, though avoiding Kingston. We found the white sands of Montego Bay and the warm transparent waters of the Caribbean as well as the variety of cocktails intoxicating. Similarly *Ocho Rios* waterfalls in which you sit as the waters sweep over and by was a fun experience, but Denise shattered my naive belief that the British Empire could do no wrong by pointing to the slums and shacks on the beach where so many lived.

We returned to Canada and life began at St Thomas High and in an apartment above Mme Lamy where we were self-contained. The year's commitment to the Montreal School Board began with pedagogical days, later adopted in England as staff study days, or 'Baker days' after Education Secretary Kenneth Baker, who introduced them rather controversially. St Thomas was situated in the Point Claire area of Dorval which was reasonably well off middle class. I was made aware early on of the structure which enabled teachers to teach a recognised plan, and not muddle through in their own way which seemed to rather precariously underpin the English education system. This was before the National Curriculum was introduced in England! Teaching was seen as serious business, rather than as a vocation. Students were encouraged to give positive feedback after lessons they had enjoyed and put forward suggestions for further lessons. The system seemed more co-operative, less authoritarian. Other noticeable differences saw a security officer on hand at St Thomas and an incredible amount of detritus in the form of half-eaten sandwiches, litter etc. left lying in corridor by 'students', not 'pupils'! Such was the affluence of society in North America apparently! The school was very large, being split between a French-speaking and an English-speaking half, each containing near a thousand students. A young priest held Mass which a handful of students attended each day. A faculty ethos was encouraged as teachers of English, History and Geography all worked together in one room under a Faculty Head. Free lessons and 'holidays' were used more conscientiously for preparation purposes. Games took the form of ice hockey, basketball and 'football', rather than 'soccer'. An Australian, John Jones, who became a good friend, and I started a rugby team and were remunerated for our labours out of school hours at year's end, quite unlikely in England. Learning in History took the form of studying European History then Canadian History and finally Modern World History in each of three years, before going on to their equivalent of Sixth Form College. Tests were invariably multiple choice and did not involve much essay writing. Canadian History was seen as dull, being mostly constitutional, compared with the other segments of the History curriculum. On return to England I adopted the Modern World History as a new and successful GCSE option. It will be seen that I got much from my year's teaching experience in Canada and it surprised me on my return that my brains were not picked by colleagues regarding the advantages/disadvantages of their schemes of education.

Life in Canada was always affected by my realisation that if I found it favourable I would likely settle there for good. House prices and such additions as basements made accommodation in Canada far superior to that in the London area for a similar outlay. However I missed what I can only term the 'quality of life', which was inferior. The theatre, galleries, museums, stately homes and castles gave great choice in and around London. Furthermore, Montreal's obsession at the time with *Les Canadiens*, that is the Montreal Canadians who played ice hockey to packed Forum crowds, was so fast that I found it difficult to follow. Athletics, cricket, football and rugby were marginalised and only Canadian football, where the Montreal Alouettes, with Sonny Wade at quarter back, won the Grey Cup that year, had any appeal. The shopping mall encompassing everything seemed to dominate in an essentially materialistic approach to life, whilst in North London the likes of Brent Cross saw this trend only just beginning. Further there was the Canadian winter lasting from November's first snowfall until the all-too-brief spring arrived in

April. Coping with 160" (13 feet) of snow was done very effectively, but even if you cross-country skied, one longed for a blade of grass long before April. The Quebec Carnival with its ice sculptures, its 'caribou' liquor drunk from hollow walking sticks, its canoe races across the frozen St Lawrence and the vast slide at Chateau Frontenac was a welcome interval, but 'Bonhomme Carnival' scarcely made up for the rest of winter's inconvenience. At the onset of snow I was dropped two blocks from Lakeshore and walked home the short distance to be told I could have been frostbitten. There was also the necessity of plugging in the car overnight because otherwise the oil might freeze with sub-zero temperatures. Once I was quite unable to start my Toyota after work in the school car park, but there were always willing hands to provide extension leads and get one started. We bought a ramshackle Ford Falcon for $100 to start with. It was of course left-hand drive, automatic and falling apart with a door hanging off. It worried me silly, especially before we got our snow tyres after the first winter's fall. Eventually Jean Pierre took pity on me and let me use a European size, manual geared Toyota which I felt more at ease with.

The one season I preferred in Canada was fall or autumn. One day a colleague offered to fly me over the Laurentian area north of Montreal in a light plane, to see the autumn colours from the air. It was so beautiful that during our return his concentration must have lapsed and he intimated that he was lost. Looking down I spied a large waterway and suggested this might be the St Lawrence. His confidence returned immediately; he had failed to notice such a prominent feature! John Jones, an Australian, was my best mate in Canada. We had similar interests in History at St Thomas and in sport. I enjoyed greatly sessions we had of two indoor games that were new to me: volleyball and handball. After these mixed games we'd go to the tavern, which was a male haunt.

Finally the end of the school year was reached much earlier than in Britain, as there were no half-terms. We decided on a holiday in Mexico, followed by our trip back, to resume my teaching career in

Britain, by the QE II. The Mexican adventure was rewarding, beginning in Mexico City with its Aztec remains, Diego Rivera murals, monastery cathedral dedicated to the Black Virgin of Guadeloupe and *mariachis* serenading us in the floating gardens of Xochimilco. We moved on to Taxco, an old silver mining town and finally Acapulco on the Pacific coast to see the extraordinary whirling dancers and experience a memorable deep sea fishing expedition with two Americans. Strapped in our seats, we hooked marlin and just as in the film of Hemingway's 'Old Man and the Sea' they leapt in an increasingly desperate attempt to free themselves. All were freed until the Americans wanted a trophy, so one was hauled alongside and given the *coup de grâce*. It was a sad moment to see its brilliant blue hue drain away, as it expired. We returned proudly flying five flags signifying the number of marlin hooked.

So we left our French Canadian relatives who had been so kind. I never did pick up the language, a mixture of modern French and 16th century French of the original 'habitants' who settled along the river banks post-Champlain and Cartier. The debate raged while I was there as to the ultimate destiny of French Canada and Parti Quebecois leader, Rene Levesque, had a strong following at the time for separation. French Canadians had a love of life, a *joie de vivre*, which came to the fore at Christmas with a round of parties lasting every one of those post-Christmas evenings, until on Twelfth Night the lights were extinguished, partying ceased and life returned to normal. It remains the country, in my experience, in which best to capture the Christmas spirit.

Nan and I.

William Field, my grandfather.

My mother Gwen Goudge, aged sixteen.

Constance Ethel Field, Gran to me.

My dad, Malcolm Field, aged 25.

My extended family at Polzeath, Cornwall, 1953.
From Right: Cousin Auriol, Aunt Elaine &
Mavis, Mother, Gran, Dad, Chris, Uncle Eric,
Cousin Maureen, Self and Nobby the dog.

Mother and Dad on their Wedding
Day June 25, 1932.

Mother, Chris, self and Dad on the promenade at Weston-super- Mare
late 1940's.

Monmouth School 1st XV 1954-55 and Coach 'Taffy' Phillips.

New House cross country Team May 1952.

Youth Hostel Badges.

6th Form at Woodford Green Preparatory School. I am fifth from left on the back row. Our class teacher the formidable Miss Read.

Mother, Dad and me by the seawall, Kennack Sands, Cornwall 1950.

Paris - in the Tuileries gardens Easter 1960.

Chris and self before leaving for Holland 1959

Chris by the statue of the boy who saved Holland by putting his finger in the Dyke. Our bikes in the background.

Before setting off on our continental YHA Tour 1958.

Camping; a cheap way of experiencing the French Riviera with Roger.

Istanbul trip with route traced out in the dust on the back of Mel's minibus 1965.

Pile up on the coach roof at the Reception for Haringey RFC on the Easter rugby tour to Elbeuf, France in 1966.

Giving the Nazi salute in the Nuremburg Stadium 1967.

With my parents on my wedding day August 10th 1974.

With Denise at the Quebec Carnival 1975.

Marlin (sailfish) hooked on deep sea fishing expedition on honeymoon, Acapulco, Mexico 1974.

Making my speech, wedding day with Denise at Lakeshore Drive, Dorval, Montreal. My bow tie has slipped, hence the joke?

Callosa, Spain 1986. Elise and an enormous bag of oranges.

Bernard and Mike by the gun on the cruiser Aurora, St Petersburg 1983. Highgate schools visit to Russia.

Denise, James and Elise in Brittany - Summer 1985.

James and Elise on the beach at Gorey, Jersey 1988.

Hofbrauhaus, Munich, August 1966. On return from Mel's trip to Italy. Note the litre mugs.

James and Elise in Spain 1994, aged sixteen and thirteen.

European teachers study tour of Japan 1985. Brian Hepple and I having dinner during our home stay with the Ishii family. Much lager beer in evidence.

My first National medal, a Bronze in the long jump. Held in Exeter, the silver medalist did not show, Tony Bateman the winner lost his face and I nearly did! We could have chosen a better photographer.

World Championships, Durban, South Africa. Medals presented by Zulu high school girls.

Left to Right: Toni Borthwick, Henry Morrison, Major Naish, Paul Ray and myself visiting Rorkes Drift on our trip to the Zulu war battlefield.

World Championships on home soil, a unique occasion. With John Ross before the 4x400 Relay 1999.

January 2003. Route to the summit of Kilimanjaro. It looks so easy, but takes many hours on the final day's climbing.

At Gilmans Point on the summit rim of Mount Kilimanjaro in the early morning sun; very cold at 6am.

July 2003 - Sign outside the Art Gallery in Ponce, Puerto Rico, reminding me of home in London.

Our 4x400 team in Puerto Rico World Championships. From left: Tony Bowman, David Burton, self and George Cheetham.

July 2004: Viking battle during a Viking Festival in Aarhus, Denmark.

With my coach, friend and rival Alan Carter in Clermont, France at the World Indoors, 2008.

With Arthur Kimber at the 1st World Indoor Champs, in 2004 at Sindelfingen, Germany.

Tony, Arthur and namesake   *Self and Alan in full flow on the bend*
Peter Field, now sadly deceased.   *200 metres.*
Ljubljana, Slovenia.

Chris, my brother, and his best friend,   *Dad with one of his final passions,*
the camel.   *a motorised scooter.*

Chapter 9

TRAVELLING EUROPE SINCE 1983

Thirteen years had passed before a school journey took me to Russia in 1983. I was now married with two young children, but the offer of a journey as the fourth teacher in a Highgate School / Highgate Wood School composite trip was too attractive to pass up. We would travel by land out and return by sea from St Petersburg. Leonid Brezhnev had died recently and Yuri Andropov headed what was to be a short-lived Communist administration. Cold War attitudes prevailed and were reinforced by a brief visit to East Berlin and by a nocturnal visit from Polish officials while entrained for Moscow. They seemed interested in what literature we were carrying, which rather reinforced our feelings that we were entering an alien world.

Bernard from Highgate School, our leader, spoke Russian and accompanying him I was able to form my own impression of Red Square and the Russian people. That given by our media at the time was hostile. Our group of some thirty students and six adults travelled by coach and was accompanied in Moscow by a Russian party guide. The 'Exhibition of Achievements of the National Economy' ranked high on the official agenda, as did Red Square. Led to expect a forbidding arena, with the beauty of St Basil's Cathedral at one end and everyday visitors and shoppers passing through, I found it anything but forbidding. We joined the queue for Lenin's tomb and the great man's waxen effigy was surprisingly small with traces of auburn hair. His aura maybe still lingers in Moscow as I was very hesitant of photographing the infamous Lubianka Prison next day. In the end I surreptitiously took a long distance view in case of arrest by plain clothes KGB! Had I read too many James Bond novels?

Our school journey group now prepared to travel overnight from

Moscow to St Petersburg, then called Leningrad. On the train, in a sleeping compartment, I found myself without my passport. Where had I put it? When had I had it last? I spent a sleepless night imagining interrogation, torture, imprisonment. Next morning as we pulled into Leningrad a senior boy, who I had been rooming with, produced my passport, to my infinite relief. He had taken it into his safe custody without informing me! St Petersburg is Russia's 'Venice of the North', more European than Moscow, and full of historical references to the Revolution of 1917. The Finlandia Railway Station where Lenin arrived from exile, the cruiser 'Aurora' that fired the shots heralding the November Revolution, and the Winter Palace stormed by Trotsky's Red Guards, can all be viewed. It is a beautiful classical city on the broad River Neva, Peter the Great's brainchild, best seen on an August evening with the final rays of the northern sun shining on the Neva and the spire of Peter and Paul fortress.

We now boarded the 'Baltika' for our journey through the Baltic and North Sea to England. Helsinki was our first stop and here we were reunited with a Highgate lad who had experienced my nightmare of the lost passport. We had left him in St Petersburg. He rejoined us in Helsinki, ashen-faced and chain smoking. Clearly he had experienced a grilling before being freed. Another Highgate boy who had been hospitalised temporarily in Moscow, where he received the best of attention, had also rejoined us before leaving Russia. Bernard took all these mishaps with little apparent concern, but his was the ultimate responsibility to parents back in England. He must have been relieved when we left Finland intact. Our final stop was in Copenhagen. From the Danish capital, the 'Baltika', an old ship built in the 1940s, was pitted against the North Sea. At times I was one of the few who dined, which surprised me as I am no sailor. Eventually we arrived, to dock in the Thames Estuary at Tilbury. It was the end of a trip of revelations for me. It had been rather like the Russian doll which still decorates my mantel, in that one inside the other, she reveals her various manifestations, all eight of them, each one of them in its own way a fresh insight.

My trip to Russia, followed two years later by a teachers' study tour to Japan, described later, made me anxious to look beyond England's shores for a summer holiday with my wife and children, now eight and six years old. My brother was part owner of a villa in the Spanish town of Callosa de Ensarria, situated conveniently behind the Costa Blanca. We flew out to Alicante, picked up a hire car and drove via Benidorm to Callosa. Part of the charm of the house was its situation and age, located in the medieval heart of the town. It had a wonderful patio on the third floor with magnificent views to the Mediterranean coast and landward to the mountainous interior. Everything that one could desire was within reach from mountain castles to river gorges, from the local mountain, the 'Penon de Ifach', to village fiestas and local *bodegas* selling local wine, strong and cheap. We were to return to this heavenly spot on three more occasions. The first was in late March and April, when Spain is at its best, with the last of the almond blossom and the meadows full of wild flowers. I arrived recovering from influenza. On 29th March we were on the beach at Moraira where girls sunned themselves topless. No better recipe for a quick recovery! James and Elise were very energetic and not yet in the argumentative teens so we walked and walked and walked in the Spanish countryside. My vocabulary is inadequate to describe these days of wine and roses. Laurie Lee does it well in 'As I walked out one Midsummer Morning', an account of his Spanish wanderings with his guitar in the 1930s. The countryside doesn't alter greatly.

The following year we descended on San Blas, Callosa again, this time accompanied by my brother and my father, aged eighty-seven. Grandad was happy to be left at the start of our walks, over the limestone heights and gorges. Remains of the Moorish period included visiting the ruins of their castles on high and Mozarabic steps into impressively deep dry river courses. Beautiful flowering asphodel covered these Elysian meads, with wild convolvulus, poppies and gorse adding further colour to the late spring display. In August 1994, two years having elapsed, we returned again. James and Elise were now teenagers and Elise brought a friend, Kelly. As they wanted to be on the beach all and every day, I left them to it, and took to the mountains and got to know the local *bodegas*. Before leaving our shores I had the vision to buy a step-by-step Spanish cookery book. I would rise early and buy at the local market, set appropriately outside the entrance to Callosa's main church. There the farmers, butchers and fishmongers displayed their wares, everything fresh and beckoning. During the course of the holiday I produced Valencian *paella, pollo al chilindron* and *sardinas murciano* and was so proud of my culinary expertise that I took photos of each and every one. My greatest difficulty was to get the youngsters to set the table and wash the dishes after our meal.

Two further episodes stand out in my memory. The first was the fiesta at the nearby town of La Nuncia. James didn't come, so I went with the two girls. In the late evening we found ourselves cowering in doorways, as villagers dressed in white from head to foot with white hoods, wheeled trolleys shaped with bull-like horns and spitting fireworks round the medieval streets. It really was quite frightening, being accompanied by screams from the two girls. The fiesta reached its climax on a stage set up in the town centre, where at midnight these figures indulged in maniacal dance, accompanied by more fireworks. This, we learnt later, was the festival of St Roque! Next morning I found the t-shirt I had been wearing was pockmarked with burns created by the exploding fireworks. It had been a memorable night. Equally memorable was the final evening, when free of culinary responsibilities, I drank too freely of the wonderful local wine and the youngsters saw me in a decidedly merry state. The wine was so good that I bought two flagons back to England. One of these surprised a well-known imbiber on the Highgate Wood teaching staff at our Christmas party, who challenged its pedigree. He ended up in a very merry condition.

Another regular holiday venue in Europe, from early days with my parents, was the Channel Islands. We travelled by ferry, or from Cardiff airport by DC 3 (Dakota) cramped and apprehensive as it lurched and rattled its way to St Helier, or St Peter Port in those early days. These were typical English beach holidays with a whiff of the continental which made them that little bit more exciting and exotic to the young mind. We grew into adults more slowly then, and my brother and I were still enjoying holidays in Guernsey and Jersey with our parents when in our twenties. I was to return to both islands with my children soon after my divorce, in one case to stay at the same hotel above Saints Bay on Guernsey that we had stayed in previously.

When the children were in their middle to late teens, becoming more ambitious, I took them to Crete where we walked the Samaria Gorge. After that adventure they became quite rancorous. Sometimes I left them to argue on the beach, and went to Knossos to view the Minoan palace excavated by Sir Arthur Evans, and the artefacts from it in the museum in Heraklion. On another occasion a day trip to the island of Santorini proved even more rewarding, as one could explore the site of the volcanic explosion which is believed to have contributed to the destruction of the Minoan civilisation. Our ship sailed into the vast bay left when the expulsion of ash and volcanic matter fractured Thera's (Santorini being its later name) symmetrical cone in several places, opening the giant magma chamber beneath to the sea. What is left is an immense bay, flanked by towering cliffs marked by lines of black, grey and pink, bearing witness to one of nature's greatest upheavals, possibly the source of Plato's legend of Atlantis. On landing, compliant donkeys convey tourists up the many stone steps to the top of the cliff where the main excavation site of Akrotiri is visited. It reveals a high degree of technical development and social organisation. Then, by a stroke of nature, Thera was gone, destroyed by the same volcanic forces that created it. It was time to return the seventy sea miles to Crete and my teenage children, bearing a bottle of the island's wine and lasting memories.

Looking back to refresh my memory of twenty years ago, I come to a memorable trip made to Spain, alone, with just my relatively new Honda Civic for company. I chose to take the overnight ferry from Plymouth to Santander and to explore a part of the Iberian Peninsula away from the 'Anglo-Costas'. The north coast is known as the Costa Verde, the 'Green Coast', and is favoured by the French for beach holidays. Inland is the essential Spain, the high flat plateau known as the '*meseta*', in August full of fields of sunflowers. This is where the best fighting bulls are bred. Would my rudimentary Spanish be sufficient to get by? Would the car let me down, for I am no mechanic?

My introduction was very Spanish with a visit to the medieval town of Santillano, west of Santander, to a gruesome exhibition on the Spanish Inquisition. There followed my first experience of the wayward, colourful, eccentric architectural genius of Gaudi in his 'El Capricho', literally 'His Fancy', in Comillas. I vowed one day to visit Barcelona where his artistry is on full display. That evening I happened on the resort of San Vicente de la Barquero, so delightful that I booked a return stop there in just over two weeks' time. The Hostal de Barquero where I stayed was part of the Chapel of the Virgin of Barquero. Tradition has it that a dismasted ship was washed ashore in the 12th century, completely empty except for a statue of the Virgin, for which the locals promptly built a little chapel. The fishing port has a wonderful setting. It has good fish restaurants and an impressive long low bridge with 28 arches stretching across the wide *ria*, to the arcaded plaza, centre of the town. This made it my favourite out-of-season resort of this Atlantic coast.

Next morning the Picos de Europe was on my itinerary, literally the 'Peaks of Europe', less extensive than the Pyrenees, but a beautiful scenic area. Rising almost vertically from the coast, they give a far greater impression of height than they actually achieve. Named by sailors in the early days of the Spanish Empire, these were the first land visible on the horizon for sailors returning after long voyages, an eagerly awaited landmark telling them that they had finally reached Europe. I drove up to Fuente Dé which is said to be so beautiful that it was the site of Paradise, and this is the Fountain of Eve. From there one can ascend by cable car to the Mirador del Cable, a superb viewpoint, and an altogether spectacular trip. Booking in for an extra day at the Hostel el Cacerio, 'Hunters Hostel', I then walked out with haversack and sunhat to explore the countryside. Buzzards with barrel wings mewed overhead and I sweated copiously as I climbed steadily to a village set with the Eastern Picos gradually shedding its cloud as backcloth. A picnic in the fields above the village, a beer later, saw me back in the late afternoon exhausted, tummy and head upset, probably due to altitude. Next day going over the Pass of the Puerto de San Glorio, I visited the highest village in the Picos where haymaking was in full swing, the hay being stored in rodent-proof huts on stilts. An American told me he was looking for bears. I didn't linger, but drove on to the city of Leon. My chief memory there is of helpings of near raw octopus eaten, but not enjoyed, in the Plaza Mayor, unlike the chorizo sausage in cider which was 'scrummy'.

To the south west of Leon lies Astorga, which in Roman times was described by Pliny as 'a magnificent city'. It is now no more than a small country town, but none the worse for that. Its inhabitants, the *Maragatos* of ancient pedigree became famous as muleteers, as Astorga was at the northern end of the road from Madrid to the province of Galicia. They cornered the transport market. Built in 1889, one of Gaudi's more wayward fantasies is the neo-Gothic 'Bishop's Palace'. This country town, like Leon, is on the *Camino*, the pilgrimage route to the shrine of St James at Santiago de Compostela. Between Astorga and Leon in Orbigo lies the 13th century 'Bridge of the Passage of Arms', said to have been the inspiration for Cevante's great classic 'Don Quixote'. A 15th century knight, Don Suero de Quinones, with nine companions, vowed to hold the bridge for thirty days in honour of his lady, Leonor de Tovar. Anyone who wanted to pass had either to swear that she was the most beautiful woman they had seen or joust. Over the following month they are said to have fought seven hundred and twenty-seven courses, broken all their lances, killed one and injured many challengers.

From Astorga it is one hundred and eighty kilometres due south to Salamanca, an elegant city of honey-coloured stone crammed with magnificent architecture: two cathedrals, a Roman bridge, university, convent, Dominican church, tower and palace. At this point I abandoned the idea of striking west through Portugal and decided to go north-west round the northern boundary of Portugal, but remaining in Spain. This route was especially rewarding in its mountainous remoteness. At Verin I felt I had reached the heart of Spain, staying just one night in the luxury of a *parador* with the castle atop the local hill, floodlit, a full moon and the inevitable fireworks until the early hours.

Next day the Atlantic west coast was reached, which I followed north to Santiago de Compostela, destination of the pilgrimage. It did not disappoint, in fact it inspired in me a wish to learn more about this journey made by hundreds of pilgrims, to the extent that I purchased a beautiful statue of a pilgrim with a traditional staff and scallop shell as a memento of my visit. Many years later I was to follow the route of the pilgrimage across Spain from St Jean Pied de Port on the French side of the Pyrenees to Santiago, a journey of over eight hundred kilometres.

The journey back along the northern coast of Spain from Corunna to Santander featured pleasant seaside resorts. La Coruña is notable for the tomb of Sir John Moore, immortalised in Charles Wolfe's poem. The city is aglitter with beautifully designed glassed-in balconies with ornamental white-painted surrounds built in the late eighteenth and early 19th century. It is known as the 'Crystal City'. The twisting Galician coastal road led to the province of Asturias, and finally to Oviedo with yet another magnificent cathedral, and a rough cider which was poured from some height, most of it falling into the glass. A local custom it seemed!

I returned to San Vincente and the ferry crossing home, during which I had a lengthy conversations with an Irish priest. This, on reflection, showed how much my stilted Spanish had limited my conversation during the previous three weeks. I was bursting to talk at length to someone about my excursion! Spain is my spiritual home as it retains so much of its historical past in its hilltop towns and villages, as well as in the cities. The cathedral or the local church retains their position as the feudal focus architecturally and socially.

I had now retired aged sixty and in August took my daughter, now aged fifteen, to Salou on the Mediterranean coast, south of Barcelona, for a week's holiday. In some respects it was an arrangement unlikely to succeed. I can now see in the wake of Jimmy Savile and similar revelations that my intention could be misconstrued. Elise said that strangers would see me as her 'sugar daddy', a factor which hadn't crossed my mind and hadn't arisen in Crete when James was with us. We decided after the first day's visit to the monastery of Montserrat, near the top of the spectacular saw-toothed mountain of the same name, that we would go our separate ways. Elise wanted a beach holiday; I was on a cultural tour of the area. This included the Gaudi architecture in Barcelona and the Roman amphitheatre in Tarragona. Towards the end of the week I took her by train to Barcelona. We visited the dramatic Olympic stadium and pool above the city, and took the cable car which crosses the port. She enjoyed that, but I blotted my copybook by losing my temper with a youth who attached himself to her on our return journey. She still hasn't forgotten the incident. Female memories are everlasting!

After retiring from teaching, what could be more relaxing than a walking week in Tuscany! My companion was another ex-Highgate Wood teacher who like me had retired as a result of stress-related depression, Tony Spinks. Tony had been the Head of Religious Education and he practised what he preached, being a thoroughly earnest and sympathetic friend. After his rather late introduction to air travel and the many benefits of Italy, he became a real lover of that country.

We were based in Siena, the most completely medieval town in Italy with its maze of twisting alleyways. Every so often they open into great squares, and of these the Piazza del Campo is famous well beyond Tuscany. Here the *Palio*, a frantic bareback horse race round the fan-shaped cobbled square, takes place. Riders represent the seventeen wards of the city. Rival processions in medieval dress parade round the piazza displaying their flags as a prelude. The action follows as it has for at least five hundred years, as the crowds excitement rises. At this point I must confess that this was March, and the race takes place twice only in July and August. However I consoled myself by buying a poster displaying all the emblems of the wards or *contradas* and a plaster memento of our *contrada* of the porcupine.

Taking a bus from Siena we arrived in San Gimignano, the hill-top town famous for its towers, symbols of the wealth of its medieval families. Climbing the 'Torre Grossa' you are rewarded with a wonderful view of the rolling countryside dotted with cypress trees. A walk beyond the town gave distant views of something akin to the skyscrapers of Manhattan Island in an Italian setting; quite unique. Our final few days were spent walking some six miles each day and absorbing the atmosphere of the Tuscan countryside. Hilltop castles, red roofs, vineyards, picnics, country churches and moody skies with the ubiquitous dark cypress is the best way I can sum up such scenes.

The Italian bug had truly bitten and in just over another year I was packing my bags for another visit to that country. This time it was to the far south, the Achilles heel, foot and toe provinces of Puglia, Basilicata, Calabria and Sicily. Under the auspices of Saga, we flew first to Bari. By chance I met an interesting lady in Daphne, widow of Professor Gordon Hamilton Fairley, a noted cancer researcher, killed when his dog accidentally detonated a bomb planted by the IRA under the car of the late Lord Lieutenant of Ulster, Lord Fraser, a neighbour. Daphne proved an interesting companion in the following weeks. This was the land of *trulli* dwellings, clusters of conical shaped whitewashed houses with grey stone roofs. I fully expected trolls to emerge. A tour of the heel of Italy took us to Lecce with Baroque architecture in soft mellow yellow stone. I remember being impressed, especially with the wealth of graceful and also fantastic images in the interior and exterior of the town's many historic buildings. The profusion of wild flowers, countless castles built on the instructions of Emperor Frederick II, and of course the food, were sources of great pleasure. On one occasion we were quite fortuitously present at the inauguration of a new Basilica dedicated to St Francis in Puolo. Signs of volcanic activity gave some idea of its cataclysmic power on Vulcano in the offshore Lipari Islands and at over eight thousand feet on Mount Etna.

In Sicily, moving inland from Catania, we crossed the island to Palermo, impressed by vast expanses of corn. Palermo is indeed a panoramic of Arabic, Norman and Baroque architecture illuminated by the extraordinarily bright light. The church of St John the Hermit is typical of this mix, with its pink floating bubble Arab cupolas and exotic monastery gardens attached to a Baroque church. The cathedral is similar in the Christian-Saracen tradition, the mosaics being among the wonders of the world. It also houses the tombs of the House of Hohenstaufen, a German dynasty of Swabian origin who wore the crown of the Holy Roman Empire, Germany and Sicily between 1138 and 1254. Frederick II was of particular note, as his interests in the temporal world of the 12th century Renaissance, and his constant anti-Papal stance, make him to me one who was far ahead for his times.

Our final visits were to the impressive Roman mosaics at the Villa del Casale near Piazza Armerina, whether of hunting scenes or bikini-clad girls, exhibiting astonishingly realistic attention to detail. Syracuse saw the ladies captivated by a handsome naval officer who showed us round his frigate, anchored on the historic waterfront. Finally we travelled to Agrigento, back on the eastern side of the island, working from one impressive Greek temple to another. With its Greek and Roman classical past we had gone back full circle. The only negative side to this Italian venture was that we saw so much, that reliving it through notes and photos taken at the time has been a tortuous experience, simply because so much was piled into two weeks. Our indefatigable courier had to escort her Saga group, ranging in age from late-fifties to the early nineties. It was hard going mentally and physically in the sometimes intense heat, so that back on the coach she had to rouse many who had nodded off, with the command to "Wake up! Wake up!", before throwing the next morsel of knowledge our way!

During the next nine years from 1998 to 2007 I travelled extensively, but to parts of the world other than Europe. However, in 2007 and 2008 the then Social Secretary of the Running Club at Trent Park in Cockfosters, Fatimah Ibrahim, ran short trips to firstly Northern Cyprus, and Iceland in the following year. It was a bonus to have someone as charming and effective as Fatimah to organise things. My memories of Turkish Cyprus are of the ancient harbour at Kyrenia and at night time of the floodlit castle and excellent seafood, squid and sea bass that we enjoyed there. The nearest we got to southern Greek Cyprus was Nicosia, where the U.N. patrolled Green Line separated Greek and Turkish Cyprus, and seemed much more relaxed than my memories of 'Checkpoint Charlie' separating Berlin had been. Northern Cyprus had given me a flavour of the island whose beautiful mixture of sunny days, swimming in sandy bays and tasty fish food with local wine, led to general wellbeing by holiday's end.

Our short stay in Iceland just four months later, for all of four days, was neither long enough nor at the best time of the year to pass judgement on the island of ice and fire. The weather at the end of February-early March was inclement. Everything was extremely expensive, especially alcohol, to the extent that we were advised to bring our own supplies of wine, which we did. Despite these drawbacks, Iceland is dramatic and worth many *krónas*. A wide valley marks where European and North American tectonic plates meet and are gradually drifting apart. Great fissures and dramatic thermal activity are the result. The Strokur geyser erupts obligingly every three to five minutes to a height of around sixty-five feet (20 metres). Nearby is the site of the ancient outdoor Parliament. One cannot help but wonder if this is purely coincidental! The Drowning

Pool, used until 1838 to punish women guilty of adultery, infanticide, perjury or any other criminal act, by tying them in a sack before being thrown into the deep pool, can be visited in this area. Finally, there is Gulfoss, an extraordinary waterfall with a double cascade, the first of a series of wide rapids, the second falling into a deep gorge. It ranks with the Victoria Falls and the Iguasso Falls in Zambia/Zimbabwe and Brazil respectively, as being the most beautiful in the world. I discount Niagara, where nature's beauty is marred to an extent by over-commercialisation.

The capital, Reykjavik, was established in 874 AD by Ingólfure Arnarson who, it is said, selected the spot in the Viking way by throwing the high seat pillar of his longship overboard and waiting to see where it had floated. At the end of four days we drove in sleet to the Blue Lagoon, a thermal lake whose warmly steaming waters were a therapeutic antidote to the raging wind. This sent us on our way home in a very relaxed manner. I should like to visit again in summer, though even then the capital receives an average of only one fine day during the month of July, a rather miserable prospect!

It had been too long since I had last visited Spain. I have already told how much enjoyment I got from a night fiesta on the Costa Blanca. Now University of the Third Age had a trip arranged to Denia, specifically to encompass all aspects of their fiesta. Of course that was not all. Culinary lessons on how to make paella and sangria and a tour of the capital of the Costa Blanca, Alicante, had been arranged. Walking up from the curiously patterned, marble palm-lined water front, Esplanada de España, the old town with its narrow streets and houses decorated with pot plants and windows hiding behind attractive wrought iron grills and lanterns, was essential Spain.

A day spent in the city of Valencia focused on the fiesta. The Falla Museum was visited. Here are kept the large papier-mâché images which were carried through the streets in fiesta since the 1930s. The winning *fallas* in the Valencian Carnaval are preserved and spared the ritual burning of the remainder, to herald spring, on March 19th, St Joseph's day. Often they are topical, satirical, colourful and always gigantic. In the Plaza del Ayuntamiente, or town hall square, we cowered among the enormous crowd gathered to see and hear the barrage of fireworks which were so powerful that the ground shook as if in a war zone.

St Joseph's day arrived and after mass at the cathedral in Denia the parade of twelve *falla* districts moved along the main avenue. The women's beautifully embroidered dresses, the fathers carrying those too young to walk, children and teenagers carrying flowers to decorate the giant Virgin and Child outside the cathedral, and music and bands were all part of the occasion. The civic pride and social cohesion demonstrated was impressive. In the evening the local fire service had to prevent trees, which had caught alight, spreading the bonfires on which the *fallas* end their brief existence, into the narrow streets.

Through U3A I was next able to carry out what had always been a dream of mine; to follow the route taken on the pilgrimage from the Pyrenees some seven hundred and fifty kilometres to Santiago de Compostela. The road of St James, or Camino de Santiago, begins for many at St Jean Pied-de-Port on the border of Spain and France and involves walking for a month or more across northern Spain. On arrival, pilgrims visit the cathedral to view the tomb of St James and probably take part in the Pilgrims' Mass. Most pilgrims travel, motivated by everything from spirituality to physical endurance, culture to curiosity.

In recent years the pilgrimage has undergone a surprising explosion of popularity as pilgrims embark on this arduous journey to search for the past, nature, self, solitude, friendship, austerity or adventure. I had tried to get others interested in accompanying me, but without success. Now I was becoming too old to walk or cycle this distance, though there are hostels along the way. In 2013 U3A again provided the answer, proposing a *camino* from hotel to hotel along the route of the pilgrimage. This was certainly better than nothing, and so it transpired.

Pamplona was our base for the first few days. Since reading Hemingway's 'Fiesta', I had always wanted to visit Pamplona because of the running of the bulls there. It was September and 'Fiesta' is set during the annual festival of St Fermin on July 7th. For a week the town goes wild. The custom of driving the bulls the eight hundred metres uphill to the bull ring goes back to the time before lorries. The streets are barricaded, to prevent the fighting bulls, weighing six to seven hundred kilos and travelling at 25 mph, from injuring the three thousand assembled. The bolder spirits jump the barricades and attempt to 'play' the bulls with jackets or handkerchiefs. The festival seldom passes without someone being gored. Pamplona is capital of the Spanish province of Navarre which until 1512 was an independent kingdom straddling the Pyrenees. After this, the ruling dynasties were as often French as Spanish. The cathedral of Santa Maria is Gothic, best seen from the back as the 18th century facade is sadly dull, best described as like 'donkey's ears on a pretty girl'. The alabaster tomb of Carlos III and his wife Queen Leonor is particularly beautiful. Carlos founded the cathedral in 1397.

From Pamplona we travelled to St Jean Pied-de-Port, literally the foot of the gateway to the Pyrenees, a distance of forty miles via Roncesvalles. Many pilgrims were gathered at the registration point for those getting the stamp of accreditation before setting forth on the first stage, a gruelling crossing of the Pyrenees. At Roncesvalles pilgrims can use the pilgrim hostel within the Abbey/Church complex to relax. Not for another two weeks, until they reach the mountains of Leon would anything be as punishing as what they had just walked. We followed the *camino* the next day to Puente la Reina, whose five-arched 11th century stone bridge, built on the instructions of a Queen of Navarre, gives its name to the town. The 'Way' then led through the town, passing noble houses with balconies decorated with coats of arms and massive doors, to the church of Santiago with a fine effigy of the saint dressed as a pilgrim. The medieval town gate used to be shut at night to keep intruders and the plague out. For our night we moved on to Logroño, state capital of La Rioja, whose wine is the finest in Spain. This is one of the main reasons for visiting Rioja. The other is that stretch of the *camino*, with its churches and monuments. Luckily for visitors it is possible to combine both easily. The church of San Bartolomé, the oldest in town, has an early 13th century facade with some lovely carvings showing the life of St Bartholomew. One of these pictures the saint as a martyr being flayed alive, then curiously with his skin over his shoulder! A visit should include at least one tour of a *bodega*, or winery, from whence comes the full bodied, slightly tawny red. The Don Jacobo vineyard had four thousand oak casks in which the wine is aged. I bought a bottle of Reserve 2004 for 10.95 Euros.

On the way to Burgos to the west, Santo Domingo de la Calzada is named after a monk who built a bridge there, to make the pilgrims' journey easier. His name is also connected to a legend which explains the many chocolate hens, hen door stops, mechanical hens, and indeed a cock and hen alive in the town's cathedral. A young pilgrim was falsely accused of stealing and hung. His parents arrived to claim his body, being delighted to find he was still alive, saved by the intervention of Santo Domingo. They rushed to tell the mayor who, irritated at the interruption to his meal, said that the young pilgrim was as dead as the roast chicken on his plate. The chicken promptly got up and started singing, whereupon the mayor realised that only a miracle had saved the youth from a miscarriage of justice. The miracle has served this small, sleepy, charming place well over the years.

Burgos by contrast is one of the great historic cities of Spain. Entry to the old city is by the Arch of Santa Maria, a fortified gateway originally, modified in 1536 as a tribute to Charles V. The hotel appropriately was full of antique furniture and art. It seemed a little incongruous to have photographs of Marilyn Monroe in the bathroom, but nevertheless welcome company for the single traveller like myself. From the sublime to the sublime there followed a two and a half hour audio tour of the cathedral. At least I made it that length of time, as it was so full of wonders, that less would not have done this magnificent building justice. The cathedral has nineteen chapels and thirty eight altars altogether. The Golden Staircase, star vaulting, family tree of Christ and tomb of Burgos' most famous son, El Cid, were a few memories I retain. The exterior is best viewed from the castle above Burgos, which the Duke of Wellington demolished in the Peninsular Wars. The fort's remains are a good vantage point to get an idea of the size of the building, its spire, turrets and towers. It is a place you will never forget. The 'Vuelta', the Spanish equivalent of the Tour de France, was streaming out of Burgos as we also left for Leon.

Leon's cathedral of Santa Maria de Regla suffers somewhat in comparison with Burgos, though its enormous expanse of stained glass is incomparable. To me, fresh from cathedrals, the Hospital de San Marcos, built as a pilgrim hospital, with a superb renaissance facade is as impressive. It is now a *parador*, but in its time has served also as a prison, military garrison, stables, and as a museum today. It has had a chequered history, but has been beautifully restored.

Rather than another full day in Leon, I took the option of revisiting Oviedo, which I had only visited briefly on my road tour previously. My memories were of cider and of a dark cathedral somehow in keeping with the city's mining heritage. Anyway, we started the day at the palace of Alphonso II built in 848 AD when the area was resisting the Moors. This involved a climb up country lanes just north west of the city. It claims to be the oldest Christian palace in the world, but was converted into a church with slender round arches well before they appear elsewhere in Europe. From its eminence there are magnificent views over Oviedo to the Picos de Europa. The fiesta in honour of its patron Saint Matthew lasts for twelve days of celebration. Its citizens clearly know how to enjoy themselves. They also keep the city exceptionally clean, garbage being collected between 8 am and 10 am every day of the week. Pilgrims are in debt to Alphonso II, not only for its wonderful pre-Romanesque churches but also because he pioneered the Northern route, which many pilgrims take to Santiago.

Finally we arrived at Santiago via Astorga and Ponferrada. Ever since my previous visit, when an American pilgrim who had just arrived at the end of his pilgrimage recounted his experience as we stood at the great west entrance, the Portico of Glory, I had wanted to spend time here. Most pilgrims enter through another magnificent way, the Doorway of Forgiveness, and thereby earn an indulgence, a tradition important to Catholics, instituted in 1122. Obradoiro Square facing west is full of pilgrims of all ages, mostly youthful, recounting their adventures of recent weeks. Many will have obtained a '*compostela*', the official certificate of completion. All will queue to pay their respects, many to show their love and veneration for Saint James. The figure of the apostle seated is dominant on the high altar, made from Mexican silver. The steps behind the altar are worn by the tread of countless pilgrims who have hugged the statue or kissed his mantle at the end of their pilgrimage. Below the statue in the Crypt a casket contains his remains.

Staying at the Hotel Puerta del Camino, two and a half kilometres away from the old town, I hiked toward what I believed was the open country, only to realise I was walking into Santiago. I found the *camino* uneven and my foot became sore. Hostels were plentiful, but make sure you have travel insurance and your European Health Insurance Card with you, if tempted. Also avoid the summer months of the 'Inferno'. Spring or autumn are the time to go.

The latest of the many European trips I have described was to the delta of the River Ebro and the Pyrenees, again in Spain. As a member of the Royal Society for the Protection of Birds, Barnet and Potters Bar section, I had long attended the meetings and enjoyed the midweek forays into the English countryside, to gardens or stately homes. An ambition to see raptors in the Pyrennees had been stimulated by TV programmes, so I joined a group led by local member, Ian Stewart, in April 2014 to that area. Our guides,

Alberto and Jaume, were to prove invaluable in identifying some one hundred and eighty-six different species over the next ten days. Our group of nine were mostly experienced ornithologists carrying telescopes as well as binoculars and cameras. They were all happy to let me use their equipment and learn from experience. Each evening we had a seminar with our guides and recorded the birds we had seen and the bird of the day, all strictly avian!

From Barcelona we drove to the Ebro delta, full of waders, egrets, gulls and terns. Flamingos were much in evidence and the black-winged stilt in the rice paddy irrigation canals were like ballerinas, so slender and graceful. The next day we seemed to visit all parts of the delta. Seeing the largest colony of the rare Audouin's gull was thrilling, and we were able to soak in the atmosphere of this wetland, a flat sponge dotted with whitewashed squat farmhouses and tall grasses.

We now drove into the foothills of the Pyrenees visiting various vantage points to see the Bonelli's eagle. Over a picnic lunch, having passed an 11th century Templar castle by in our quest for the eagle, we were rewarded with excellent views of a Short Toed Eagle cruising by the cliff. Distant views of Bonelli's and various larks, but not the elusive Dupont's lark, followed. The phrase 'up with the lark' was certainly appropriate as next morn we left at 6.15 am, driving out to bushy scrubland to listen to the melodious call of Dupont's lark in the gradual dawning. By 7.30 am when the sun rose, sightings of this first bird in the dawn chorus had been rare. It is the bird which sings first in the pre-dawn, so it doesn't have to compete, as the light comes, with the song of the more common larks.

The next day was probably the best for birding on our way to the High Pyrennes, as we saw a Golden Eagle and, at a canyon, a brilliant view of an eagle owl. Bee eaters and little bustard reminded me that we were not too far from Africa. In the Pyrenees' foothills now, searching the crags for the rare wallcreeper, we were rewarded with Griffon and Egyptian Vulture and Lammergeier. Birds of Britain which I had never seen, like the Wryneck and colourful Dartford Warbler, were found, as well as wild dark bee orchids and Spanish festoon butterflies. Back at the Boletas, our tour company's hotel in Laperzano, we were treated to the sight of house martins nesting, as well as a cream of courgette soup provided by Esther our hostess. It was so delicious that I purchased her recipe book of homemade treats. The afternoon of the next day took us to yet another cliff face in our quest for the elusive Wallcreeper. After an hour and a half of patient watching we were rewarded with fifteen minutes viewing of our target bird. Jaume, our guide, was elated and kept crying out "I love you, Wallcreeper!"

Our final days were spent in the High Pyrenees, reaching 1802m above sea level at St Martin de Pierre ski resort, just across the border into France. Here Alpine Chough and Ring Ouzel complemented the Firecrest seen at close quarters in the hotel grounds. We drove up to the Monastery of San Juan de la Peña. Lunch was taken, and a much needed walk took us to the Revilla viewpoint for magnificent close up views of Lammergeier cruising by, not far above us on the thermals. It was a wonderful sight and fitting climax to the holiday. On the final evening Esther delivered spaghetti in garlic pesto, followed by a mixed grill of lamb, sausage and chicken with jacket potatoes and salad in a garlic mayonnaise sauce, followed by strawberry cheesecake. So you see it was not only the birds that I remember!

Chapter 10

FATHERHOOD

Denise and I returned from Canada in the summer of 1975. We travelled back in some style on the QE2. At first we stayed with my previous landlady, Mrs Finnissey, in a fairly spacious upstairs bed sitting room in Crouch Hall Road, Crouch End, London N.8. Denise obtained a temporary position nearby as Assistant School Secretary at Highgate Wood School. I resumed my position as Head of the History Department there. My wife had been used to the relative luxury of the large house on Lakeshore Drive, overlooking the St. Lawrence Seaway. Living in 'digs' was understandably little more than a short term solution until we found our first home in England.

In 1976 we took out a mortgage on a three bedroom house in Brookside South, East Barnet, about four miles from the school. Denise had some furniture shipped across from Canada, and we acquired some from my parents' home in South Wales. Before long my wife began a course at Trent Park Teachers Training College, Cockfosters, Hertfordshire, toward the necessary Certificate in Education. This would enable her to teach her subject, Art, in England.

Shortly after we had moved into our new house, the Olympic Games took us back to Montreal for a time. It was not a successful Olympics from a British point of view. The people of Montreal did not want it, and with the single exception of a Japanese vaulter, I cannot recall any competitor smiling or seemingly enjoying themselves. We saw some sports that I had played for the first time in Canada, like volleyball and handball. After the Games, a trip to Canada's Maritime Provinces provided a rare sight. Off Bonaventure Island, from a small open boat, we saw flocks of gannets retracting their wings and diving into the sea to catch fish. It was an image so swift that I failed to capture it well on camera, but if remains etched indelibly in my memory.

On our return to England I was soon engaged in constructing built-in wardrobes in the new house, to be followed later by a new patio. Do-itYourself projects are not really my forte and I grumbled at length, and showed myself to be generally ham-fisted, though the result was acceptable. In contrast I enjoyed greatly making home-made wine from the apples of our solitary tree.

As a relaxation from our weekly work we visited parts of England new to both of us, like Lincoln and Chester, and had a delightful skiing holiday at Lermoos near the Austrian border with Germany. This was in the company of Keri Davies and his wife Joan, whose wedding in Yorkshire had been in the same year as ours.

It was Silver Jubilee year 1977, and our first child was on the way, quite unplanned and unforeseen. A new washing machine was purchased, a scan revealed that a boy was expected, baby clothes were acquired, pre-natal sessions attended, and on April 8th 1978 some weeks before he was due, James Malcolm Field arrived prematurely. I was selfish enough to resent being unable to play rugby that day, in order to assist with his birth, in the labour ward of Chase Farm Hospital in Enfield. After some time in intensive care, Jamie came home and Denise's mother, Madame Lamy, arrived from Canada to join my parents to celebrate the new arrival. The yellow broom was in bloom in the garden. In late May Jamie was christened at the Church of Christ the King, Cockfosters, and the priest, Dom Joly, joined us in the garden afterwards, holding the baby under the apple tree. Thereafter, progress was charted in a series of photographs taken until, at eight months, he travelled to a Canadian winter in Montreal. A return to further snow in East Barnet in February 1979 saw him take his first steps. Summer 1979 saw the idyll continuing with a holiday on the wild coast of Northumbria. This included a boat trip to the Farne Islands, full of seabirds, above all the countless puffin. Bamburgh Castle was where my son failed to appreciate the reverential atmosphere expected within such historic monuments and turned the occasion into one of saving face. Dunstanburgh Castle was in a position so exposed and bleak on the coast that there were no tourists to upset! With Lindisfarne on Holy Island and its associations with early Celtic Christianity and Berwick's magnificent walled fortification, the wild North East is an historian's dream.

Family life was complete with the arrival of Elise Germaine in November 1980. An interesting interlude came when we inherited a caravanette, or camper van, from friends of Denise, who had used it to travel to Europe before returning to Canada. It took us on weekend visits to Essex, and to Naseby and Bosworth battlefields in the Midlands. It finally expired in the West Country when Denise joined her younger brother, Jean Louis, touring with our children, and I never saw it again! Three memorable summer holidays in the West Country between 1980 and 1982 saw us based at Polzeath, Cornwall, Fowey in Devon and again at Polzeath with my parents and Chris. Jamie and Elise were the focus of our attention and activities during these days, as we saw them in their joyful years of innocence. In the years which followed we explored the coast of Brittany, staying for two years running in holiday villas. The first at Ploneour Lanvern took our breath away when first we saw it. Up a long curved rough track, in the middle of a meadow full of buttercups stood a large gabled residence with shuttered doors leading onto a sun drenched patio. It was the stuff of our fantasies. The following year's residence had to be an anti-climax, but gastronomically the scampis compensated, the fish food dinners being exceptional in that part of France.

At this point some reference should be made to the only time in my life that I owned a dog. This was a black and white pure-bred pedigree spaniel. Unfortunately rather like the human species, interbreeding resulted in a loss of intelligence. The career of Charles II of Spain, poor man, whose death was expected at any moment during his reign, is a case in point. Eventually, his demise resulted in the catastrophic War of Spanish Succession. But I deviate. Boo, for such we christened our dog, certainly lacked brains, but this deficiency only caused minor inconveniences. Denise had always had a dog and Elise wanted a puppy. I bowed to their wishes, providing they trained it and walked it. Neither happened on a regular basis. To compound Boo's and our misfortune, he was left alone all day, so went mad with joy on our arrival. At this point if I took him for a walk he had a habit of rolling in faeces, sheep's for preference, or having an argument with a larger dog, often in the hands of a teenage minder, unable to control it. A near fight would ensue, from which I had to extricate Boo. He was hardly my best friend.

In November 1985 I was chosen with eight other teachers from Great Britain and Northern Ireland to go on a three-week study tour of Japan. Earlier I had entered a written submission on why I should be one of the chosen, mentioning that I taught a fair degree of modern Japanese history in my modern world course to GCE. I was somewhat surprised, but delighted, to hear that I had been success-ful. The entire trip, air fare and hotel expenses would be funded by Japanese Airlines.

The successful applicants met in the Imperial Hotel, Russell Square, for a sort of Japan initiation day. We were urged to visit a school which taught Japanese, take lots of presents and read up on Japan. I remember reading James Clavell's "Shogun" and another book aptly titled "The Chrysanthemum and the Sword" which gave some insights into the Japanese psyche.

As this was in term time at Highgate Wood Comprehensive, my colleagues agreed to cover my classes, otherwise I would not have been released. We flew out via Moscow arriving at Narita Airport, Tokyo on November 2nd. I was impressed initially by the skyways - a vertical traffic system leading into Tokyo above ground level. This consisted of busy motorways carried over other roads, to ease congestion. At the time, only the North Circular at Brent Cross was a pale imitation of this.

The first day of our week in Tokyo was for sightseeing, so we visited the Imperial Palace, seen from afar in wooded seclusion across a bridge spanning a serene water course. The huge wooden Buddhist/Shinto shrines and pagodas, the slim smartly attired female guides each with their flag followed by a gaggle of tourists, and the ordinary Japanese going through rituals of infant baptism before Shinto priests and homely rights of water purification and incense burning, were evocative images.

Next day we visited Waku Private School. We were always given a very formal presentation before touring classrooms and other facilities. We would then foregather as a group of European teachers and have a discussion, for they were at pains to point out that they wanted to learn from us. One of our number, previously deputed, gave a formal closing thank you. Presents and addresses were often exchanged with the children, one of whom continued a correspondence in copy plate written English with accompanying photographs for quite a time after my return.

In Tokyo we also visited Kabuki traditional theatre, the smartest shopping area, the Ginza, and Expo '85, then being held there. At one point a couple of Sumo wrestlers, enormous guys in traditional blue and white robes with a stomach sash, their hair tied in a tight knot at the back, strolled past.

It soon became time to leave Tokyo, so we caught the *shinjuku* or 'bullet train' on the 9th November for Nara Prefecture which was to be our area of study, including Kyoto, city of a thousand shrines. On this train journey through industrial development, past paddy fields and terracing for tea growing, we caught tantalising glimpses of Mount Fuji.

Our first school visit in Nara was to Koshiba High. Class sizes were larger than in Britain. The extra-curricular activities held after school were admirable, including flower arrangement, calligraphy and judo. As honoured guests we were treated to a tea ceremony and I was picked as our representative. It is a very delicate ritual performed by a beautiful girl in a floral kimono before not only our lot, but the tea ceremony class and Japanese TV. I'm told I appeared in all my very clumsy twirling of the cup etc. on TV that evening. Fortunately perhaps, I never saw this. At Unebi-Higashi Elementary we arrived to lines of youngsters clapping in a rather formal way, but left to a more spontaneous applause, having received gifts of origami, juggled bean bags and marvelled at the size of the swimming pool and activity area.

Our next experience was to be entertained by the Nara Education Board at a *ryokan* or Japanese inn. For this we donned Japanese robes and sat with legs stretched out (under low tables) on the floor; after a time this can become an excruciating form of torture to the westerner. After the banquet with much saki and lager, the school board gave us a hearty *banzai* which I had seen on newsreels of Japanese kamikaze pilots. I assume it means 'farewell' for proceedings ended fairly abruptly at this point.

So that we saw the full range of schools, we next visited Gojo Kindergarten and finally our one journey into the interior took us to a mountain school which was more informal; a band among the trees, one of our number crowned "king" for the day, playing of scissors, paper etc. Now came a memorable experience: the home stay with a Japanese family. In our case it was three generations of the Ishii family. Brian Hepple and I slept on futons, removed our shoes on entry, took the obligatory bath before eating and were entertained to a wonderful meal served by Mrs Ishii and her daughter, whilst father, son and grandparents maintained the conversation in English, assisted by much lager beer liberally served by the ladies. At one point we arrived at the customary giving of gifts. We had been instructed in London to take something typical of England. For some unknown reason I chose to take an English cheese, which gradually matured as our trip progressed. By the time I handed it over to the Ishii family it was so smelly that I felt very embarrassed, but went ahead anyway. As ever the Japanese were very gracious, but what must they have thought of this ripe object?

From Nara it was but a short journey to Kyoto with is wealth of temples. Nijo Castle was built for the first Tokugawa Shogun around 1606, as well as shrines and *toriis* (ceremonial gateways). What impressed me most were the beautifully decorated interiors and the ornamental gardens so tranquil and calming, often with golden carp in the lakes, rocks and water lilies.

Finally we went to Hiroshima, forever associated with the dropping of the atom bomb in 1945. The peace museum had horrific reminders of that fateful day. From there we visited one of the many success stories of post-war Japan, the Mazda car plant, and were impressed by the extent to which the process of assembly was in the hands of robots.

All too soon it was time to return to Tokyo for our flight home and fond farewells, especially to the other members of our British group. We had shared a lot of good evenings together in karaoke bars and sushi counters. Later we had a reunion in Ramsbottom, Lancashire, whence came Brian, one of our number. My only memory of this is being taken to Bury, black pudding capital of Britain, Brian proudly proclaimed.

Later I was so captivated by Japan that I applied for a job with the British Council, but was turned down on grounds of age, for I was fifty at the time. On reflection I came to the conclusion that our invitation was really to the advantage of the Japanese, as we all returned to our respective schools with tales of our wonderful time, which after all was good publicity for Japan among our younger generation.

Chapter 11

Running in Britain, Europe and World-wide

When I left Birmingham I temporarily put aside my running interest for rugby, which involvement lasted for the best part of the next twenty-five years. Finally, aged forty eight, a knee ligament injury ended my rugby career and to strengthen the knee I took to running up stairs. The distance running boom had begun in the early 1980s with the London Marathon, so in 1985 I joined a small group of teachers from Highgate Wood School preparing for the London marathon. One of them, Dave Willett, had drawn up a list of preparation races, including half marathons, a twenty mile road race and a ten kilometre. The last two were to be final preparation, to be run two months before and a week before the marathon respectively, to test distance and speed. The road race at Bury St Edmunds, Suffolk was run on a bitterly cold day over an undulating course. It was so cold that the water was freezing in the paper cups and there were flurries of snow. Perversely perhaps, these conditions were ideal, once warmed up early on. I finished in two hours, forty one minutes and was given a predicted marathon time of around three and a half hours.

The great day, 20th April, arrived. A train journey to Blackheath for the mass start saw us across the start line after five minutes, and all was well until Tower Bridge after eleven miles. Only then did I begin to feel that our thirty miles a week training was inadequate. The section round Canary Wharf and the docks was hard going. On the cobbles by the Tower of London I cramped up and needed some self-massage. The crowds on the Embankment and down the Mall were a helpful incentive, though the headwind was not. I finished on London Bridge in three hours, fifty four minutes, well over the prediction, but satisfied nonetheless.

This began an obsession with distance running which lasted fully nineteen years. During this time I ran sixty half marathons, twenty-four full marathons, twenty-one ten kilometres as well as six twenty kilometres. These events took me to all corners of south east England and in the case of marathons to areas well beyond in Britain and Europe. Training by running established local routes was a cathartic experience after a stressful day's teaching. It felt good to be alone and free of pressure, pounding the streets of suburbia or the adjacent country roads. Towards the end, the wet and dark winter evenings took their toll and I joined Trent Park Running Club for companionship after many years of running and training unattached and solo.

Many are the memories and mementos from these days. At the Glasgow marathon I was on track for that elusive predicted time, but as ever the final six miles were the most testing. Though I ran three hours, forty-five minutes, my personal best, as I staggered across the finish on Glasgow Green a kindly volunteer offered me a wheelchair! The Land's End Marathon was the hardest event to complete. I arrived at Land's End in mid-April, aged fifty-two, for the marathon. Only a hundred and twenty runners were assembled. On enquiry I found that in the previous year many had ended up in hospital with hypothermia. It was a tough course along roads parallel with the north Cornish coast, then across the moors to the outskirts of Penzance and back to Land's End again. The weather was wet and cold. Finally I came within sight of Land's End, in some desperation now. A motorist, sensing my plight, gave me a pac-a-mac, which proved my salvation. I finished seventy-ninth out of the eighty finishers in a minute under four and a half hours. For some time after, despite frequent hot drinks, I could not stop shivering. In retrospect, I realise this was probably hypothermia. Somewhat restored, I then drove back to London. It had been an eventful day, marked not by the customary finisher's medal but by a certificate, which to this day means more to me than any medal.

In October there followed a stark contrast involving combating the heat and hills of the Athens marathon. Starting from ancient Marathon on the coast, the course ran for six miles fairly flat, then for a prolonged gradual climb of some fourteen miles, before dipping down into Athens, to finish in the original marble-built 1896 Olympic stadium. One reached the top of the climb with some relief and looked forward to a gradual descent. It was at this point I realised that I had expended so much energy on the climb that there was nothing left in my legs. I walked and jogged the remaining miles, so today I can claim to have finished a marathon that Paula Radcliffe failed to complete! However in the Athens Olympic marathon, Paula was running much faster and in much hotter August conditions, so there is really no comparison. Nevertheless, when I see pictures of her withdrawing from the race, I like to think in some small way that I know how she felt. October is the best month for marathon running as it never gets too hot and the colours of autumn are often at their very best at the end of this month. The most scenic marathon I experienced was the Seven Sisters, starting and finishing in Eastbourne in the final week of October. I ran it twice at the end of my "career" of distance running, in 1994 and 1995. You can add probably about an hour onto your usual marathon time and I finished in over five hours each time. This is because it is run over country rather than roads. You are taken through delightful villages, Alfriston being the best example. The course finishes, just when you are at your most fragile, with the formidable challenge of the Seven Sisters, each one involving a climb, which you have to walk, being too exhausted by that time to run. Finally there is Beachy Head, another small matter of five hundred and thirty-six feet above Eastbourne. On a sunny day, as it was in 1995, nothing could be more intoxicating.

Each marathon has its own character. Malta is run downhill from ancient Medina in the centre of the island to Sliema on the waterfront. One expects a good time as a result. My time was not as good as I had hoped. I explained to the guy who shared with me that my sleep was affected badly by pre-race nerves. He said that he took

Night Nurse, a cold and cough treatment, to make him sleep the night before. He must have given me a double dose thirty-six hours before the start. I not only slept like a log, but kept dozing off the day before. At the start at 6am, I still hadn't recovered, and it took me ten miles to banish the effects and start running freely, hence a disappointing time.

The Berlin marathon, just a few days before the Wall came down in late September 1990, was memorable for a number of reasons. Part of it was run through East Berlin, the Russian sector of the city. The Berliners there, not having seen westerners for decades, looked at us as if we were aliens from a distant planet. With only one hill of any note, it is probably the fastest marathon course in the world. It finishes down the Kurfürstendamm, the main thoroughfare, with jubilant crowds urging the runners to a final effort. The reward came at the end, when one queued for a massage by not one, but two, very beautiful German *fräulein*. Finally there was Dublin, my second fastest marathon, completed in three hours, fifty-three minutes in October 1988. The entire weekend was programmed by Aer Lingus and my memories are threefold. There was the impressive architecture, a pint of real Guinness and finally the two urchins who offered me a sponge outside a tenement block, soaked in dirty water. Just what I needed at that point! However it's the thought that counts! Quite a contrast to Berlin and also the Rotterdam marathon, where fruit was bountiful. You maybe see how running marathons is a great way of gauging a city's mood or temperament.

Now came an event that that was to change my running life. Recently having joined the Trent Park Trotters running club, every Thursday evening's run with the older members consisted of hanging on to the rest as we went up the long slow inclines of Beech Hill in Brookmans Park. We would then end our seven mile route by the shorter, but more vicious, Cat Hill in Cockfosters, before returning to shower at the local cricket club. A then-member of the running club, John Denford, was more interested in promoting Track and Field athletics than in distance running. He organised, as a social event, a pentathlon, to be run, thrown and jumped at Queen Elizabeth stadium, Donkey Lane, Enfield. Entering, though somewhat apprehensive about my throwing powers, I knew I could compete in the 100 metres and long jump. The final event was the 400 metres in which for my age, then nearly sixty, I ran a creditable sixty-three seconds, beating someone rated quite highly. A club member, Mike Miller, came up to me after the race and suggested that I could make an impression in veterans' athletics at that distance. This was news to me as I did not then know of the existence of national and international, club and area Track and Field for so-called veterans. This term was eventually americanised to masters and lowered from age forty to age thirty-five. I decided there and then to find a coach and give it a go.

A good friend, Toni Borthwick, was "making waves" at middle distance running and was a few years older than me. I approached her coach, Paul Ray, who was also a race walker, of similar age. He explained that he wasn't a sprint coach, but that I could train with Toni and he would do his best to advise me. His coaching experience was invaluable, and when in 2003 I eventually won the European championship 400 metres in San Sebastian, Spain, it was with an imaginary Paul on my shoulder, urging me on. But there was a long road lasting many years before that day finally arrived.

It began in the summer of 1996 when the three of us travelled to Exeter for the National Championships. We stopped on the way to enjoy Toni's homemade scotch eggs and arriving in Exeter made a beeline for the track. Toni remembers finding it looked much further round than the usual 400 metres. This reflects the fact that we both felt terribly nervous before our first big championship. Next day, 28th July 1996, Toni broke the world record for 800 metres for her age group (60 to 65 years old) by a staggering 9.5 seconds, recording 2 minutes 54.5 seconds and winning gold, running against much younger people. I won a bronze medal in the same category, jumping 4 metres 41 centimetres in the long jump. Paul ran a hot bath for me as a reward, which from him showed a high level of approval.

Our first big competition had been a great success and you always remember that first big success as special, as much as one remembers the first county or area gold medal.

We now needed to move on to world level, so in July 1997 we three arrived in Durban, South Africa, for this experience. For me the athletics were less memorable than other events. On the fifth day of our stay my suitcase in the hotel room was broken into and most of my currency was stolen. It was fortunate that my passport and credit cards had not been targeted. Next day we had arranged a trip to the Zulu war battlefields, north of Durban. Major Paul Naish (retired) of the Rhodesian police force's opinion of the inhabitants at the time was as uncomplimentary as mine, still smarting after the recent theft. We were shown the battlefield of Isandhlwana with its memorials to the slain and also a panoramic view from the escarpment above. The battle was expertly relived from both viewpoints by Major Naish, after which we moved on to Rorke's Drift. In 1879 this was little more than a mission store and hospital. After the massacre of British forces at Isandhlwana, five thousand Zulu warriors attacked those beleaguered at the Drift. Laagered behind hastily erected sandbags and biscuit tins the garrison resisted the *Impi*, to the extent that more Victoria Crosses were awarded to the defenders than in any other single engagement in British military history.

The next day Toni won the world 800 metre event and her gold medal was presented, as were all the medals in the championships, by bare-breasted Zulu high school girls. Rather more than the usual number of photographers jostled at the medal ceremonies! In the evening of the following day the athletes' party was far and away the best I ever attended. Nelson Mandela had been released from Robben Island and was in control in South Africa. A group led by Sharon Katz and called the Peace Train, comprising young children of primary school age, joined us on the dance floor. They turned and twisted among us to the song "We are the children of South Africa". It was heady stuff which I still play to this day, when in need of emotional reawakening. I had my turn receiving a medal on the final day, when our British 4x400 metre relay team finished third, a full length of the straight behind the first two teams. To make up our team, a javelin thrower and a jumper had been included, so perhaps this result was not so surprising.

I left immediately after the championship on the Garden Route along the coast of Cape Province from Port Elizabeth to Cape Town. The scenery of cliff, cave and coast was dramatic. My parents had spoken in glowing terms of it. Indeed at Wilderness, a wide bay of rolling seas, my father had rescued a swimmer in difficulties, mother had told me. Moving inland to a dry plateau dotted with acacia and pepper trees, we entered the Little Karoo, for me the most unfamiliar and interesting part of the trip. Ostriches are farmed here for their meat and feathers. Oudtschoorn bore every sign of having been prosperous in pre-war days when ostrich feathers were so fashionable. Now it was simply the largest town in "Thirstland", the Hottentot meaning of Karoo, a wide landscape of bare mountains and scrubby plain.

In February 1998 at Kelvin Hall, Glasgow I raced indoors on a track which has recently been replaced. At the time I found it less impressive than the National Indoor Arena at Birmingham. This was an under-statement. Its hills and dips would not have been out of place in the Cairngorms! All my events were concertinaed together on Saturday. In the long jump and 200 metres it was a thrill to win national bronze medals. The final event was the 400 metres. This I won by using the final steep descent to just pip my long-term rival, friend and present coach, Alan Carter, on the line. It was a well-judged tactical victory according to what I wrote at the time, but Alan debates that to this day. The gold medal was presented by Henry Morrison who was to become a friend and with whom I went to Tanzania five years later.

I had really "got the bug" by now, and in September of the same year arrived in the Italian fishing town of Cesenatico, between Ravenna and Rimini, for the European championships. Everything about the next ten days was a new experience; the savoury food, friendships formed and an interesting trip made to Rimini. Inland beyond San Marino lay San Leo to which four of us travelled using local buses. It had been recommended by an Italian friend from the running club and like most Italian hill towns it was a gem. I suppose I was on a high, having just come fifth in the final of the 400 metres after a good run, following a night when I slept not at all through nervous apprehension. A personal best (PB) of 61.35 seconds shows how adrenaline can compensate for sleep deprivation. Two days later in the final of the 200 metres I improved to fourth position which, it is said, is the worst place to finish, as it is just outside the medals. On the final day I medalled at last with silvers in both the 4x100 and 4x400 relays. It was a great feeling to have arrived successfully on the veterans/ masters track scene. Ten races in eight days left me feeling quite exhausted and a short trip to Venice came as something of an anti-climax, surprisingly. I have a beautiful multi-coloured fish paper weight in Murano glass to remind me of those few days. The organisation of these championships was very good, so much so that I wrote afterwards to the Italian responsible, especially compliment-ing the efficiency and good humour of two girls I had got to know. In the call room where the runners are marshalled before racing they persisted in calling me Field Colin which seemed to amuse us all.

The next World Championships were held in England at Gateshead in July 1999, lasting twelve days. Away from the athletics I was able to visit the church where my grandfather had ministered, inspect records of his death and funeral in 1927, and visit Bishopwearmouth cemetery, Sunderland, where he and my gran are buried. Everyone in nearby Sunderland was very helpful and without their assistance I would have got nowhere. In addition Paul, Toni, Gina, a walking protégé of Paul's, and I visited Beamish Open Air museum, Housestead's fort on Hadrian's wall, and Durham Cathedral. In this way we felt we had had a snapshot of this part of the North East through time. We stayed in Collingwood College, part of Durham

University. The BBC were making a film, later entitled "Old Gold", about veteran athletes. Toni was under siege from then, which made Paul rather irritable as he felt it was a distraction from the real business of performing. She ran well in the 1500 and 800 metre finals, but had a nasty fall pushing for a medal in the 400 metres. My best moments came in the relays where Alan Carter, John Ross, Tony Bowman and I pushed the Germans and Americans hard for the medals, finishing each clearly ahead of the other national relay teams in bronze medal position. It had been a superbly organised vet-Olympics though the food drove some, including myself, to seek better fare in a nearby pub. Driving into Gateshead from Durham each day, on extensive trips, and to and from London, was taxing and Toni's admonition of "Steady, Colin!" was a regular refrain. In summation one has to wonder why no further World or even European Veterans/ Masters championships have been held since in Britain. The facilities, especially since 2012 with the new Olympic stadium at Stratford, are custom-made for such events.

From reading so far you might think my obsession with running is a story of unmitigated success. Nothing could be further from the truth. There are noteworthy seasons and threadbare times of injury or illness. Fortunately when injury intervenes, physiotherapists can often help. The British team could fall back on the experience and knowledge of Steve Peters, himself a top rate Masters athlete. Fiona and her team of physios and masseurs have more than once strapped me up so that I could at least function, for which I was very grateful. If you are unable to run at all there are at least foreign, often exotic, locations as an alternative to day after day watching others compete. For me Finland has not been the best of venues. In 2000 in Jyvaskyla I reached a European semi-final and a final, neither of which I was able to run because of an ankle problem. Nothing is worse than seeing your name go up in lights on the giant screen and then being unable to race. The solution is to go canoeing on the lake and to experience a real sauna in a shack by that lake before immersion in its ice cold waters.

Back in the Finnish capital, Helsinki, six and a half years later, my jinx struck again, when a pulled hamstring in the final strides of the 60 metre indoor final of the Europeans caused me to miss the rest of the meeting. Having had a massage on the previous day proved to be bad medicine, as it always has been in my experience. Yet some athletes seem to spend more time being pummelled by masseuses than actually running. A few days later, an acquaintance from Haringey rugby days, Nick Burton and his wife Ann, drove me to the ancient capital, Poorvoo. It was in marked contrast to the capital, with cobbled streets and a house, now a museum, in which the composer of the country's national anthem had lived his last twenty years. This restored my equilibrium nicely. Running and foreign travel balance out well very often, as there are always days free of competition when one is at liberty to explore beyond the stadium.

My journey to Australia in 2001 was completely unbalanced in favour of exploration. Breaking the flight to Brisbane at Singapore, the Botanical Gardens with its famous collection of orchids was just the beginning of a memorable six weeks. The National Museum makes an excellent introduction to the history of the port, whose modern skyline does its reputation justice as key to Australasia and the Far East. A gin sling in the long bar of Raffles Hotel was followed by the long overnight flight to Brisbane. The world championships were held in the Anzac stadium, home of the Queensland Reds rugby league at the time. A fortnight before, I had had a muscle spasm in the final yards of the national 200 metres at Eton. Although I got through a five kilometre fun run in Brisbane, disaster struck a few days later in the 200m heats, when the strain in my rectus femoris insertion meant that I lost a lot of power and was eliminated. Strapped up later for the 4x400m relay, in which the British team finished fourth, was my only other running experience.

I had not come that far for nothing however. Visiting a koala sanctuary, the Gabba cricket ground and the Australian Woolshed to witness all things woollen, was at least an attempt to empathise with "Down Under". More exciting things followed. One day Paul and I boarded the "Cat O Nine Tails" for St Helena convict camp, named after an aborigine thief named Napoleon. There, actors playing the roles of a tough warder and a prisoner marshalled us and recreated effectively the atmosphere on this prison island, housing some three hundred and fifty prisoners, finally disbanded in 1933. The actors did a realistic job of showing how brutal, hard and wretched life must have been for the prisoners.

A day was spent whale watching and then I flew to Cairns where we boarded a massive catamaran at Port Douglas for the Great Barrier Reef. It was a day to relish. A safe area had been set aside, off a promenade in the ocean, for snorkelling. The fish and coral were so colourful and beautiful in what was an underwater paradise that it excelled any other such submarine areas I had ever visited. It was one of those days which remain in the mind forever, an eleven out of ten day, as I recorded at this time. A cruise in a small boat up the Daintree river followed next day, in which we saw many waterfowl and amphibians, including dragon lizards and large estuarine croc-odiles basking in the sun on the sand banks. At a day at the fair in Cairns, Henry Morrison and I witnessed pig racing and bush poets declaiming their verses; both were thought typical of Australia. The pigs jumped obstacles and bets were laid.

After all this and more in radiantly sunny Queensland, we did not get the best weather in Sydney. Winter in the southern hemisphere includes Christmas day celebrations in July and holiday weather the further north you travel. Even in the middle of their winter however, Bondi beach and Sydney cricket ground had atmosphere. One regret was when I 'chickened out' of the climb over Sydney harbour bridge, which I have heard since is well worth doing.

Henry by now was on his way home, but I had arranged to spend a few weeks in New Zealand, so flew on to Auckland, a three-hour flight from Sydney. The idea was to hire a car and drive round North and then South Island, visiting on the way three friends from vari-ous times in my past. John from Auckland, who I had met recently in Serengeti Game Park, Tanzania, recommended Kelly Tarlton's waterworld, where you experience rays and sharks swimming above and around you and the superb view of the city from Mount Eden. Westhaven marina claims to be the largest in the world and the city breathes yachts and the America's Cup. As in Brisbane, the National Maritime Museum gives a fine introduction to the history of North Island.

Hiring a car was not difficult, though I felt some trepidation when given snow chains to use if necessary. So I left Auckland, driving north to the scenic Bay of Islands, roughly where the first settlement was made around 1350 when many canoes arrived, probably from Tahiti. The settlement of Russell was New Zealand's first capital and was reached by ferry. The carefully manicured lawns in front of the treaty house in Waitangi heralds the place where the treaty of that name was signed in 1840 with the Maori. A recreation of a Maori war canoe, rowed by some one hundred and fifty oarsmen, can be seen. This area is matchless in scenery and is the focal point for the creation of a nation. Driving back south again I entered the Coromandel Peninsular, another area of outstanding natural beauty. Andy Pettit had been a hero of my schooldays at Monmouth, where he played scrum half for the First XV when I used to watch from the touchline. He and his wife Ruth lived in a cosy home with an orchard of tangerine trees beside. We had real honeycomb at breakfast and the best lamb ever tasted that evening. Next morning Andy took me to see a grove of kauri trees in the remote forest. These trees are becoming increasingly rare and are some of the oldest in the world, around six hundred years old! In the nearby bay, called Cook's Beach Bay, lay a three-masted sailing ship. It could have been 1769, when the great navigator first mapped these shores.

From the Coromandel I drove to Rotorua with its Maori heritage and spa therapies emphasised in the town museum. At Whakarewarewa I enjoyed a Maori concert, although commercialised, put on by locals with traditional singing and dancing. Later I bought a Maori wood sculpture of the carved head which usually adorns the apex of the barge boards of the Maori *whare,* or meeting house. Some have large owl-like eyes to keep watch over the marae or sacred place, and a protruding tongue which is an attitude of defiance in the face of the enemy. The thermal activity in and around Rotorua ranges from colourful mud pools, craters and blowholes to caves, terraces, waterfalls and geysers which spout every so often. The so-called Polynesian pool, a set of pools of varying temperature certainly gave me a very relaxed night's sleep. The little church beside Lake Rotorua had a statue of Christ etched in the window glass, so that if viewed from a certain angle he appeared to be walking on the water, which I thought very clever.

Napier on the West coast was interesting, with claims to be the Art Deco capital of the world. It was rebuilt largely in the early 1930s following a massive Richter 7.9 earthquake. Nowhere else can you see such a variety of buildings in the styles of the 1930s, above all Art Deco and Spanish Mission, enhanced by palms and pines. My final date on North Island was with Greg Cardin, a New Zealander who had taken my place in the Haringey rugby team in the early 1980s. Greg greeted me in what he explained was New Zealand fashion, with a bear hug, when he met me in Wellington. The superb Te Papa (Our place) museum on the waterfront and a quite strenuous windswept walk to the top of Mount Victoria, for a fine view over city, airport and harbour, explained the city's nickname of "Windy Wellington". Greg was a great host and I responded in local fashion by giving him a bear hug when I left Wellington next afternoon by ferry for South Island.

Cook Strait can be stormy, but the crossing to Picton was relatively calm, enough to admire the scenery of Queen Charlotte Sound. Next morning a longish walk on the Tirohanga Walkway behind Picton gave me a stunning view of its natural harbour. My way now took me through the Buller Gorge to Westport, where Greg's niece had a house. She had said in Wellington that the key would be underneath a stone and I could let myself in and stay. Such is the habit in New Zealand. Driving along the west coast of South Island was a wonderful experience. It is, to my mind, the wildest, most natural and scenic coastline in the world, completely uncommercialised, with a pleasing uncluttered road running conveniently its length. You can take in colonies of seals, beautiful sunsets, and at Punakaiki the Pancake Rocks, as well as Franz Joseph glacier further on. Punakaiki is one of New Zealand's smaller national parks. Les and Deborah managed the park, which was the site of a tragedy in 1995, when a viewing platform collapsed over a creek, plunging fourteen students and a guide to their death. It was hard to imagine this in such a 'garden of Eden'.

Around the Franz Joseph and Fox glaciers the rain, never far away on this coast, set in, and the road turned inland over the Haast Pass. Were the rain to turn to snow I would have to find someone somewhere to fit my snow tyres. My prayers were answered and the rain did not turn to snow. The lakes and high snow-capped mountains were very picturesque hereabouts and at Wanaka my charming hosts at the bed and breakfast booked me on to Te Anau and a coach to Milford Sound. Most of my overnights were spent at bed and breakfasts, much more hospitable than motels. Without exception, their owners were friendly and helpful. What with the lack of traffic on the roads, the friendliness and the slower pace of life, New Zealand reminded me much of England in the 1950s.

Moving on towards Queenstown, home of all sorts of extreme sports, I passed through the gold rush centre of Arrowtown and in the museum learned how badly the Chinese miners had been housed and treated. A meal of green-lipped mussels in Te Anau that evening was special. Next morning my coach to Milford Sound picked me up. We drove the most wondrous route stopping at rushing streams, mirror lakes and the site of tree avalanches. When we stopped, the cheeky kea, a native parrot, attempted to vandalise our rubber windscreen wipers. This bird can be a pest, but much indigenous wildlife had been wiped out by foreign birds and rats. The kiwi is now very rare, the giant ostrich-like moa gone generations ago. Aboard the sailing ship "Mariner" we had a wonderful cruise past

Mitre Peak into the fiord, with spectacular waterfalls and enormous granite cliffs down which numerous cascades tumble. Rainfall here is measured in metres, around eight per annum, making it one of the wettest places; it rains two days out of three, but the rain and mist add to a unique atmosphere where our boat was miniscule in comparison to the forces of nature.

After Milford Sound, travelling on to Dunedin and north up the east coast of South Island was largely an anti-climax, until Oamaru. Here numbers gathered to see yellow eyed penguin coming out of the sea, and the smaller blue penguin, who emerge once it is dark. On South Island at times you feel close to Antarctica. Flying home took thirty-six hours from Christchurch to Sydney to Singapore and finally London, with six hours in Sydney. No wonder New Zealanders feel a mite isolated and welcome people from the "old country" with open arms.

In August 2002 running took me to Berlin. Unlike my visit nineteen years previously on my way to Russia, the Potsdam area where I stayed and competed was now part of a united Berlin in a united Germany. Frederick the Great's palace of Sanssouci (without care) and the Cecilienhof Palace, where the momentous Potsdam agreement was signed by the wartime Allies in 1945, satisfied my historical interest. The 400 metre final taught me to never ease up until you have gone through the finish line. Thinking I had the bronze medal, suddenly I was aware of the German competitor, Horst Hufnagel, crashing to the ground, having dipped on the line to my right. Dr Hufnagel was a good friend who made a practice of hugging me prior to competition. I didn't feel much like hugging him at this point, as he had deprived me of my first European medal in an individual event. I was to have my revenge the following year, and we did gain silvers in both relays, which was some consolation. As in the 400 metres, this was behind the Germans, who are always very strong in Masters' athletics wherever the competition is held.

On January 24th 2003 I climbed to Gilman's Point on the crater rim of Mount Kilimanjaro. Mention of this is relevant perhaps to winning the European 400 metres six weeks later in San Sebastian, Spain on March 9th. Altitude training or living at altitude is known to benefit athletes, though mostly distance runners. The meeting was compressed into just five days. On the first morning it transpired that the 200 metre heats had been brought forward a day, quite unbeknown to me. I had eaten a cooked breakfast when fellow athlete, Terry Bissett, surprised me with this information. We rushed to the stadium, signed in, and ran the heat. Afterwards I felt a bit sick as my breakfast choice was certainly not the best preparation. The semi-final of the 400 metres next day saw my friend Arthur Kimber and Horst beat me, by overtaking me on the back straight during the second lap. Nevertheless I qualified, and was surprised to hear that the two very good Germans in the other semi-final had withdrawn, to save themselves for the 200 metre final. On the next day I won the final of the 400m by making sure I was not overtaken again down the back straight, and getting ahead of the other two at the end of the first lap. The 400 metres indoors is run in two laps and the tactics are to get ahead and stay ahead, coasting the bends in the final lap, when overtaking is more difficult. In the short finishing straight I had enough left to hold on for the win. Arthur was second and Horst Hufnagel third. I'm sure the climb up Kilimanjaro gave me the speed endurance needed. Later we scooped the silver in the 200 metre relay which, with the medal ceremonies, rounded off the best day of my life in track running.

Later in early July of the same year, 2003, the World Championships were held in Puerto Rico. The island of Puerto Rico is categorised as a territory of the United States ever since it was annexed from Spain as a result of their war in 1898. Vestiges of Spanish rule included the entrance to the harbour at San Juan, the capital, where the fort of El Moro resisted every attempt at conquest by the Dutch and English in earlier times. In most other respects Puerto Rico is americanised, to the extent of having a casino in our hotel. At Ponce, on the island's south coast, the Art Museum housed a fine collection of paintings, especially strong on the pre-Raphaelites. A phrase from Keats' "Endymion" caught my eye at the entrance: "A thing of beauty is a joy forever". Suddenly in this far off tropical island, hot and wet with warnings of dehydration and sunstroke, I was back in Enfield, North London and Keats' House, Hampstead where "the cockney poet" had lived his short remarkable life. On my return I entered a competition which required a quote from Keats and why said quote had had an effect on me. I won the competition with an explanation of how this line had brought me literally down to earth in a foreign land.

A year later, in July 2004, the European Championships took place in Aarhus, second largest city in Denmark. Getting towards the end of the sixties age group and with an ankle which had to be strapped up before racing, nothing of note was achieved on the track. A Viking festival saw the Danes brandishing shields, swords and battle-axes storming into conflict, helmeted and waving flags, many riding small ponies bred in Iceland. In the tented encampment, amber necklaces, birch bark and leather work, as well as fox and coyote fur hats, were displayed. Though it rained, it did not spoil a splendid battle which drew a vast crowd of camp followers, a few of whom spoilt the illusion by raising umbrellas! In Aarhus museum I saw the authentic Viking collection of weapons and buildings. The most interesting exhibit however was the contorted face and body of a man's remains preserved in a peat bog, known as 'Grauballe Man'. He was probably a sacrifice from time immemorial, stunned and his throat slit. Old Aarhus displayed over fifty craft buildings from the past with todays' local children and adults dressed in period costume in peaceful quiet settings. Finally we took a trip to the far north of Denmark where the Skagerrak (North Sea) meets the Kattegat (Baltic) at Grenan. A swim in the latter sea was cold, but very invigorating. It was also noticeable how Denmark, a flat country, was using wind power in a big way, wind farms being a major feature of the landscape. I find they're only marginally more disturbing than windmills of old.

We now move on two more years to Poznań, Poland in the summer of 2006 for another European competition. Unlike the professional athletes, Masters fund their own trips to events and there is no selection policy. Readers will have noted by now that European and World Athletics Championships for Masters athletes occur in alternating years, so there is scope for competition at a high level against athletes of similar age every year, with the proviso that one has the necessary funds. It has to be noted that as a result of this, competitors from the better off nations proliferate, whereas Africa for example, apart from South Africa, is under represented.

Poland at the end of July was extremely hot and with no covered stand for spectators, all sweltered. Our British relay team won bronze medals in both relays. The medals depicted two goats on one side. At various hours of the day, models of these city emblems appear and butt each other so many times according to the hour, above the city hall clock. The city's life revolved around the main square, restored after extensive wartime damage. The city's coat of arms features a pelican, symbolising rebirth of the nation after partition. The first kings of the Poles are buried in the cathedral on the island in the River Wart where the city was founded in 968 AD, being Mieszko I and Bolesław I, the Brave. Modern Poland has homely touches, statues to old Maryck with cycle and a Bamberg woman on her way to the well, rather than to warriors of old. Its cuisine is positively earthy, e.g. half a duck with apple, red cabbage and potato dumplings, or beetroot soup followed by potato casserole with salmon, but as such essentially Polish. It was our particular joy to eat Polish in one of the many open air Polish restaurants in the medieval square, whilst watching the girls pass by on the warm summer evenings.

The antics of dolphins at the athletes' party, 6th century Romano-Byzantine mosaics in Ravenna, the Ducal palace in Urbino, prototype of the urban community; these were a few of the lasting memories of twelve days in Riccione, Italy in September 2007. Again a World Championship bronze medal, finishing behind the Germans and Finns, was added to a mounting collection. Our Best

Western hotel was a delight, the waiter Marco a consummate comedian who was expert at filleting a fish in the blink of an eye. On the final evening, two of us visited a lap dancing club and left in the early hours before we spent a fortune.

2008 was one of the more successful years in terms of athletics. The World Indoor Championships were held in March at Clermont in the Puy de Dome volcanic area of the Auvergne, France. Reaching my first world final in the 60m, I finished fifth in 8.83, a time last achieved eight years previously. Clearly the winter spent doing a session of plyometrics, flexibility exercises, as well as circuits once a week, had been beneficial. In the 4x200m relay we gained silver behind old rivals, the Germans. The city was notable for its cathedral, in whose square a statue of Pope Urban stands, where he gave his blessing to the First Crusade in 1095. Further back in time, the Frankish chief Vercingetorix's victory over Caesar is commemorated by a monumental statue in the Place Jaune. Climbing the many steps to the roof of the cathedral for a fine view over the city, on my return I had difficulty in letting myself out. The concierge had let me in to the tower, perhaps he had inadvertently locked me in. In semi-panic I forced open the heavy door and fled.

Sometimes a venue turns out to be better in all respects than one's expectations. Such was certainly true of Ljubljana, capital of Slovenia. Situated on the upper reaches of the river Sava it is more provincial than most capitals. Its restaurants, spread along the riverside, offered tasty fare and everything of note was in easy walking distance. Typical of the homely nature of Ljubljana was a 19th century painted board used as a front to a beehive. It told the biblical tale of Solomon judging between the rival ladies as to who was the legitimate mother of a baby, but in a 19th century peasant context. The lady's baby is about to be sawn in half, and the reactions of the onlookers betray their feelings. It was claimed that six hundred different "beehive fronts were being applied", no pun intended! A visit to the stud farm at Lipice to view the white horses which perform in the Viennese Riding School was also noteworthy. They seemed gentle, graceful creatures seen in their historic stables and in the fields. The athletics was a mixture of disappointment and success, as it often is. Having qualified as third fastest for the 100 metre final, I strained a groin muscle in the warm up beforehand, and finished last. However all was not lost and by the end of the week, judicious application of ice had done its work and I finished a good fourth in the 200 metre final as well as gaining an enormous glass medal as the bronze in the 4x100m relay.

A brief trip to Ancona, Italy, for the European indoors again showed how a disappointing campaign sometimes ends on a reasonable note. The weeks leading up to the event were ominous with visits to my foot specialist, the excellent Asha, to treat a pressure ulcer and provide cushioning. I teamed up in Ancona with Jack Fitzgerald, a veteran walker who sympathised with my foot condition and who moved around at a suitably leisurely pace. He had won a bronze medal in his event and done a lap of honour in front of the admiring crowd. Later that evening he told me that he had been to Ancona before.

"When was that?" I enquired.

"We bombed the place during the War" he replied, "but don't tell the Italians, will you".

For my part I kept his secret and went on to gain yet another bronze in the 200 metre relay, thanks to Eric Horwill, another walker, who made up our team of patched-up sprinters.

Earlier in this chapter on running I told how Finland had proved an unlucky country for me. This changed in 2012 when a return visit to Jyvaskyla twelve years later for the world indoors proved more successful. The town is in the Finnish lake district which is unremarkable, as Finland, rather like Canada, is a very watery country with countless lakes, iced over in winter. Arriving by air at Tampere, the temperature on April 2nd was -3 Celsius. A very smooth train journey, lasting a couple of hours through miles of snowy coniferous forest brought us to Jyvaskyla. We then tramped through the snow-bound streets until we found the magnificent Skandic hotel. Within the first four days I came fifth in the 60 metre final and seventh in the 200 metre final with good times. The elevated track only accommodated four lanes, so in the 200 metres there was an A and a B final, the result being judged on times.

The next day, in order to relax, I went on a Finnish evening which gave an insight into traditional Finnish life with a buffet of authentic Finnish food, dancing, music and singing. It was held in a fine log house. The oldest British competitor, Mary Wixey, in her early nineties, agreed to be placed in a traditional crib or cradle to be photographed in the spirit of the evening. The following evening sampling deer and elk stew followed by tar ice cream, unique to Finland, I was invited to Montreal, Canada, all expenses paid, for a week of testing at McGill University. Professor Tanja Taivassalo was recruiting athletes who had reached world finals for a research project on "Superior Aging: Lessons from the Masters Athlete" at the university's Muscle and Exercise Research Laboratory. It was a wonderful opportunity to return to the city where I had been married and did my teacher exchange thirty-seven years before. Prior to this however there were the London Olympics to enjoy and then the European Outdoor championships in Zittau, Germany in August.

I was unable to get any tickets for the Olympic Athletics either in the general public application or in the very limited number issued to my running club, Trent Park. Making the best of it, I enjoyed beach volleyball at Horse Guard's Parade, foreground to a London skyline stretching from Nelson on his column, holding an Olympic torch, to Westminster Abbey and the London Eye. In Ripley, Surrey, my cousin Auriol and I got soaked in a thunderstorm watching the women's cycling road race. At Wembley stadium, the semi-final of the women's football tournament between Japan and France was a revelation, with no histrionics and skilful play. The mood of the crowd was typical of cosmopolitan London throughout the Olympics, being good natured and happy. "An Hour with Haile Gebreselassie" at the Criterion Theatre was quite revealing, as was the exhibition of Olympic memorabilia at Covent Garden Opera House. Later on I captured the spirit in the stadium at Stratford on a September evening of Paralympics when the eighty thousand crowd were treated to a cloudless sky and some extraordinary performances.

I do recognise at this point that recollections of my lifelong interest and participation in athletics, especially at the Super Veteran age, will begin to pall for many. By the time my coach, friend and mentor Alan Carter and I journeyed to Zittau, Germany in August 2012, I was seventy-six years old. Having had pleurisy earlier that summer it was not surprising that I made little impression in the sprints, other than in the 4x100m relay where our team collected our now familiar European bronze behind the familiar Germans and Russians. Zittau was not far from the Czech border, being but a brief walk down the road from where Alan and I lodged in the Alte Schmeide, a charming Tyrolean-style pension. We were some distance outside Zittau and the only bus in passed at 6.30am and the only bus back departed at 10pm and left us with a lengthy walk back. Despite this Alan collected a gold in the 300 metre hurdles and two European bronzes in the sprints. He may have done even better had we not got legless at times through the amount of walking we needed to do in the rugged countryside.

Our cuisine was an interesting mixture of Slav and Teuton, for example Czech garlic soup, pork chop, sauerkraut and dumplings or goulash stew in red wine, wild mushrooms and the inevitable dumplings, followed by a berry compote. The town's prize possessions were two Lentern Veils, used to cover the alter during the forty days of Lent. The larger one dating from 1472 is one of the most impressive textiles in the western tradition, over fifty square metres in size, and depicting the biblical story in ninety pictures of scenes from the Old and New Testaments.

Earlier in 2012, as previously recounted, in Finland, I had been invited to Montreal for a week of testing at McGill University. The purpose of the study was to determine what factors permit high physical function in advanced age by comparing 20 Masters athletes to 20 healthy individuals of a similar age who were not highly active. Participants for the study had to be seventy-five or older and in the case of the Masters athletes chosen, to be still competing and to have placed amongst the top 5 in one's age category at a recent international Masters Athletics competition. Two other British athletes as well as Canadian, American and Spanish athletes had accepted. We were sent a consent form and lengthy information about the testing procedures outlining the nature of each test, its demands, benefits and any possible risks. An option to withdraw at any time was given.

So on October 15th 2012 at 7.30am Arthur and I met Tanja, the Principal Investigator, in the entrance to McGill University. We began with a heart echocardiograph which determines the size, shape and functioning of the different chambers and valves of your heart. I had to hold and exude breath whilst the young French Canadian doctor made a record of the heart's response. I had never heard my heart pounding away rhythmically like an engine and this was to me a unique experience, as was seeing the heart working. After an hour or so I was told that all was well, though I did have a small valve leak, which is not unusual.

Whilst Arthur completed what appeared to be a tough exercise test on a stationary bicycle, which I would do on the day after tomorrow, I filled in a series of questionnaires covering lifestyle, physical activity levels, background and demographics, physical and psychological health and motivational factors.

I then moved on to Magnetic Resonance Imaging (MRI) of muscle and brain, which uses a strong magnetic field to allow study of the function of the brain. I lay on a table which glided slowly into a large tunnel, open at both ends. Any fear of claustrophobia was dispelled as one could communicate with the operator, who if necessary could be seen at one end of the tunnel. The machine made a loud knocking sound when images were being produced. I had to remain still during the sessions over a period of 40 minutes without falling asleep! Having taken pictures of my head I was repositioned to take pictures of my thigh muscle for a further stationary 15 minutes. So ended our first day.

Day 2 was just the one 45 minute test to measure the activity of muscle groups in the lower leg. Small needles were inserted and surface recording electrodes attached which enabled patterns of muscle activity to be examined, providing information about the neurological control of the muscles. We completed muscle contractions from very mild up to maximal effort and then concentrated on maintaining a steady level of contraction for a given period.

The third day was the most exacting. For the VO2 max test I was wired up by Norah ready for various heart monitoring and breathing tests, before mounting the bike. The resistance on the pedals was very low at the start and got harder every two minutes until I felt the need to stop. Further, I had signed a separate consent form agreeing to an evaluation of how my diaphragm responds to exercise. I had to swallow a long thin tube inserted through my nose by Cassandra and fed down the oesophagus leading to the stomach. The tube was secured to my nose with tape and I was required to wear a mouth piece. I looked and sounded a bit like Darth Vader! The test became quite hard after about 16 minutes. One had to maintain a spin speed of between 60 and 80 on the bike. If it fell below 50 the exercise was stopped. I came close to 200 which got the onlookers urging me on, quite excited, as up to then it was higher than others had reached. I'm pretty sure it won't remain that way.

In the afternoon I had to perform a constant work - rate exercise test at between 40 and 70 % of the peak heart rate achieved in the previous test. My heart rate, breathing and blood pressure continued to be monitored. Electrodes attached to my head examined the flow of blood to the brain. This took over an hour with two breaks. Samantha, a highly organised young lady wearing heavily rimmed spectacles, who I christened the Professor, gave me an hour or more of cognitive function tasks as determining attention, memory and decision making. This was as mentally challenging as the morning's physical challenges.

At the end of the day Sylvie, Tanya's organisational aide, took me to the back of the university and showed me a route up Mount Royale which I walked in the wonderful colours of the fall to get views from on high of the city spread beneath.

In the evening Arthur and I, two female athletes, Olga aged 93 and Christa aged 75 from Vancouver, and two Montreal cyclists, Harold (80+) and Murray (75+) also being tested, were taken to a splendid Montreal restaurant where many connected with the study were met, including Bruce, who had written a book about the remarkable Olga.

On the penultimate day a machine called the Biodex measured the strength and endurance of calf, thigh and hip muscles. I had to kick as hard as I could and then for as long as I could, both from a seated position. This was followed by some balance exercises, timing of runs up a short flight of stairs and hand grip tests.

For the final day we had to fast from 8pm the previous evening, and next morning had 50ml (approximately nine teaspoons) of blood taken. There followed DEXA or Duel Energy X Ray Absorptiometry, basically a small dose of radiation from a full body scan, followed by a detailed spinal and hip scan. Later we moved to the muscle biopsy conducted by Dr Jose Morais, a Portuguese who put me at ease by claiming he would samba to my choice of background music! It involved removing a small piece of muscle from my right thigh for analysis. The spot was numbed and a nick was made with a scalpel to make an opening for the tubular pencil-shaped biopsy needle. The needle was inserted about 5cm into the thigh and a piece of muscle was removed. The muscle sample was then analysed for fast and slow twitch fibres. It was interesting to see one's own muscle fibres. Later I watched, having assured them I was not prone to fainting, and suitably masked to ensure a sterile environment, whilst Arthur had his biopsy. Proceedings continued with a visit to the gym where we did single bench presses to a maximum weight and multiple lifts with about half the weight, bicep curls and body pull ups, all measured. Finally to the university indoor 200m track for a photo shoot with the others for an article in the Montreal Gazette.

We were then left the best part of the weekend to sightsee, travelling by metro to the 1976 Olympic stadium, Botanical Gardens and Old Montreal as well as shopping with the $300 Canadian allocated over and above every other conceivable expense being paid for. On the Saturday evening a dinner party hosted by Tanja and her husband Ross, with traditional Ukrainian fare prepared by Olga, was enjoyed.

In March 2013 almost to the day, ten years after winning the European indoors 400m event, I returned to San Sebastian for another European Championship. Winning the customary bronze in the 4x200m relay behind Germany and Italy, but ahead of Portugal, Russia and Spain, the achievement didn't rank with that of ten years before. Nevertheless Track and Field's David Barnett provided his company's itinerary for the World Championships in Brazil later in the year, which I was to follow up. In addition a rugby game in an adjoining stadium between two French sides, Bayonne and Toulon, was very entertaining. A team mascot masquerading as a horse, riding a motorbike and then a skateboard, added to everyone's amusement after the Basque side's tries, by circling the pitch in crazy fashion. The afternoon was memorable as few matches at the highest level are in England, but then I am a fan of Welsh rugby!

So in mid–October, just before Britain shuts down for winter, I left Heathrow bound for Sao Paulo, Brazil and the Masters World Championships in the south of the country, at Porto Allegro. There were twenty-eight runners entered for the over-75 100 metres. I reached my first World outdoor final through heats and a semi-final and finished sixth in the World final out of the eight finalists. Coach

Carter was fourth. We celebrated in the evening at a Brazilian athletics fraternity party, courtesy of Alan's brother and sister-in-law. The sheer energy and acrobatic skill of the dancers, whom we joined, made this a uniquely Brazilian experience. Next day in torrential rain on a flooded track I failed by 0.1 of a second to make the 200 metre final when my legs turned to jelly in the final twenty metres. Perhaps this was the result of the previous evening and only four hours sleep. The next day was one of triumph for Alan who was all over the local paper having won the 300 metre hurdles and finished third, one ahead of old rival Tony Bowman, in the 200 metre final.

I enjoyed the rest of that day with Tony in a gaucho tack shop where we drank yerba mate or green tea through the traditional metal spouted vessel, going on to a gaucho restaurant. Here cooked meats on spits were removed and piled on our plates using evil-looking knives until we pleaded for them to stop. The floor show featured an act in which *bolas*, the gaucho lasso, was spun thrillingly and manipulated with precision. A trip on the local lagoon in which Tony and I, with our American friends, were joined by pink-clad young cleaners out on a works spree, and the local beauty queen, reinforced the impression that Brazilians know how to celebrate. Unfortunately there is the other side of the picture, that of the favela slum and crime. My first view of Tony had been earlier as he had passed by in a police vehicle, his camera having been stolen. The rather pretentious Continental hotel nearby was robbed at gunpoint.

During our excitement on the lagoon I had been stung by a bee and, being allergic, I had received an injection in the buttock to reduce the swelling at the First Aid tent in the stadium. The injection of dexamethasone was a steroid, on the banned list of drugs, one of our team doctors informed me, so it was as well that my competition was over.

The flight to and from Brazil was very long and expensive, so I now transferred arrangements from Track and Field to Trailfinders, who had mapped out an interesting itinerary for me to follow after the athletics. From Sao Paulo I flew to the Iguassu falls where Leonardo awaited. That afternoon he took me to the Parque des Aves (Bird Park) where an exotic range of colourful toucans, flamingos, parrots, macaws, all saved from destruction, were on show in spacious conditions. To me the scarlet ibis and the menacing harpy eagle were most photogenic.

It is difficult to find words suitable to describe the world's most powerful waterfall in terms of water flow per second. The Iguassu Falls are indescribably beautiful, without the commercialisation of Niagara. Like Victoria Falls, their natural environment is also part of their attraction. The variety of butterflies is astonishing; lianas and epiphytes create a mass of vegetation. Swifts drop into the mighty abyss of the falls and black vultures wheel overhead. Leonardo enabled me to see the falls from the Argentinian as well as the Brazilian side. From the former, a raised catwalk links islands in the Parana River, leading to a raised balcony, known as the Devil's Throat, from which the 1100 metre long view of the biggest fall can be experienced. A similar walkway below the falls on the Brazilian side leads to an amazingly intimate view of the enormous volume of water involved. For this oilskins are advised as the spray is considerable. In all there are between one hundred and fifty and two hundred and seventy waterfalls!

Now I flew to Manaus, a flight lasting close to three hours which emphasised Brazil's size. On the Amazon in Manaus I boarded an Amazon Clipper, not unlike a Mississippi riverboat, designed to dock at remote spots and access difficult locations. Some interesting trips by canoe were made during the next three days, mainly on the Rio Negro, in the dawn or in late evening by using torches. We saw a wide variety of birds and reptiles. A close up view of a bird eating tarantula and volunteering to hold a two year old caiman were personal highlights. Luiz our guide felt that I was holding it too tightly! Jungle craft included how to make a blow pipe with curare–tipped arrows, how to kill an attacking jaguar and how to make fire using just a stone. On the final day we fished for piranha, watched pink dolphins and visited a village where the business of converting manioc into bread or pancakes was demonstrated.

Finally I flew out to Rio where my hotel room had a fine view over Copacabana beach where soccer volleyball, skateboarding, cycling, jogging and walking tiny dogs seemed popular pursuits. Visits were made to the impressive 120 foot statue of Christ the Redeemer at altitude 2,400 feet, bestowing a blessing on Rio's inhabitants, and to the Sugarloaf for a panoramic view of the entire city. It is a place of infinite variety and is quite magical, fulfilling one's expectations. Samuel Johnson said of London, we Londoners are fond of recalling, that "if one tires of London one tires of life". The greatest compliment the good doctor could make to Rio is that it is precisely that in the modern world.

Up to now my near obsession with running has taken me to many rewarding locations, the latest of which, in 2015, was Lyon in France. Here the World Championships were held and it proved another interesting location, not least because it has the reputation of being the gastronomic capital of France. It is also very easy to reach nowadays by Eurostar and once there has an enviable uncluttered metro system. Our residence was near the station 'Monplaisie Lumiere', so called because the Lumiere brothers developed moving pictures there in the 1890s. Their attractive palatial house is now kept as a museum celebrating their invention. Lyon's museums are located in buildings themselves of architectural or historical interest. The Musée Gadagne is a sumptuous Renaissance structure in the lively narrow streets of the Old Town, and it does an excellent job of outlining the city's heritage from Roman times to the present. The Musee des Confluences, situated where the Rivers Rhone and Saone meet, had four galleries in a beautiful modern structure. The exhibits are wide ranging from fossil dinosaur eggs to a Brochier wedding dress. It is a thoughtful place which draws the crowds.

The area around Lyon also proved rewarding. Annecy with its pastel coloured houses and church on an island is a charming place with an impressive natural lake. The Lac de Monteynard is an artificial lake beyond Grenoble with turquoise waters and views of the distant French Alps. Chartreuse is famous for its green liqueur made from countless herbs, flowers, honey and ginger which remains a secret concoction.

My final day in Lyon was spent in the Resistance museum housed in the old Gestapo headquarters. I saw a macabre film outlining evidence given at the trial of Klaus Barbie for wartime crimes, including the deportation of children to Nazi concentration camps. It left a nasty impression, partly dispelled by the work of the French Resistance featured in the rest of the museum. Let us leave the final memory of Lyon to the table. Not the delicacy of this part of France which is sausage made from offal, but a salad gourmand with pate de foie gras, tarte tatin and a pot of the local Beaujolais.

Now, at long last you say, we arrive at an explanation for the title of this biography: 'Run for your life at 80.' It is a reference to my success at the World Championships, Track and Field for Masters athletes, held between October 26th and November 6th 2016 in Perth, Australia.

With my 80th birthday arriving on July 14th 2016 I saw this as maybe a final chance to compete at the start of an age group, namely the 80 to 85s. Training hard through the summer under the expert guidance of coach Alan Carter I arrived in Perth with a sheet of notes on how to approach each race in heats and finals of the 100 and 200 metres. In his 'preparation' notes Alan had written, "you have trained hard the last couple of months and I know I have pushed you, but you have hung in there. You can do it; remember the determination you had in San Sebastian, that's what you need with you as well."

During the twenty-hour flight from London to Perth, I watched films on Jesse Owens and Eddie 'the Eagle' Edwards which were motivational. My initial reaction to Perth was that its architecture was modern, with wide streets and absence of pressure. I soon found a Jamie Oliver restaurant and felt at home. Next day an excellent rail system and then a shuttle bus conveyed me to the stadium, where I did a warm up routine with caffeine sachet before and recovery bar after. I had packed ten of each of these in my track kit bag to allow for all preparation and race sessions.

The first two nights saw me get little sleep as I was jetlagged badly. Fortunately the adrenalin surge one gets before and during a race seems to compensate and I got through my heat in second place in the 100 metres in 16.50, a time well inside what I had been doing back home. The prevailing wind, nicknamed 'the Fremantle Doctor', blowing at +1.9 velocity certainly helped. The track had been aligned to take advantage of the wind and was so sacrosanct that needle-sharp spikes were forbidden. Next day at 1pm we went to our marks for the final. Making my usual good start, concentrating on running relaxed and tall I was in position for a medal until the final metres when Bob Cousins, an American, and a Norwegian finished stronger to register 15.65 and 15.64 in third and second places. I finished fourth in 16.09 with a German fifth and Czech sixth. The winner was Tony Bowman in an astonishing 14.85. The 'Fremantle Doctor' blew hard at +4.7, far too strong for record purposes, which need to be in a wind of under +2.0. The photography after and during the race was brilliant, with many images of the races in which I ran available for purchase. Satisfied that I could brag now at being the fourth fastest eighty year old in the world, I slept well at last!

The next two days were spent in light training. Local landmarks were visited like the Bell Tower which housed the original 16th century bells of London's St Martin in the Fields, once rung to celebrate victory over the Armada and at Trafalgar, now rung over the city of Perth. The mint, in whose melting house gold from the 1899 Gold Rush was cast, and the famous WAACA cricket ground, also received attention. Latterly, the second day consisted in resting in preparation for the 200 metres the next day.

Tuesday November 1st dawned sunny, a typical Perth day in springtime. Unusually both 200 metre heats and final had been timetabled on the same day. In the heats held at 9.10am I ran conservatively as a consequence and finished third, only just qualifying for the nine-man final in the early afternoon. Between races I relaxed in a quiet spot. In the final, though starting much stronger, I finished seventh in 36.95, which was over two seconds faster than my previous season's best. After the 200 metres there were a number of days left for sightseeing and watching others perform until November 6th, when I ran in the British team 4x100 relay. This was an anti-climax as Rod Mills, our third runner, had injured himself in the 400 metre final earlier, and was really in no condition to run.

In the intervening time I had made trips to the Pinnacles, an area well to the north of Perth, studded with tall limestone pillars, the remains of compacted seashells subsequently eroded. Another short sea journey from the port of Fremantle took me to Rottnest Island, home of a friendly marsupial, the quokka, at first mistaken by early settlers for a rat, hence the island's name.

With these memories of my most recent running adventure, which I deem a success, it seems a suitable point to finish this chapter of my life. I have decided to continue running competitively for another year or two, and to adopt this title for my biography, as it encapsulates nicely my chief interest, among many, in my life at eighty years of age. The title also sums up my philosophy of life, which is that life is to be enjoyed in as full a way as possible for as long as possible. Indeed, that with the benefit of greater experience and more leisure time, life is often easier and more rewarding than ever to manage as one ages.

Chapter 12

YEARS TO REMEMBER AND YEARS TO FORGET

The 1980s was not my happiest decade. Mother passed away in 1985 and two years later Denise instigated divorce proceedings.

Both of our children went to Monkfrith primary school, situated conveniently at the end of our road. Oakhill Park with a children's playground, tennis courts and lots of open space was only a short walk away.

You will recall that in 1984, with Elise aged four and Jamie six, we decided to cross the channel to Brittany. We returned to Brittany again the following year. This time we took the car ferry to Normandy, visiting the Mont St Michel, the monumental prehistoric monoliths at Carnac and the Normandy beaches at Arromanches. The oldest calvary or representation of the crucifixion was visited in a churchyard in Tronoen. Jamie loved seafood and is pictured with Elise before the largest plate of scampi I have ever seen.

These good times ended abruptly in 1985 when my mother passed on after a lengthy battle with breast cancer. She had had a mastectomy six years before and the disease returned in 1984. Dad moved her bed into the lounge front room at Castle Street, Usk, and there I visited her, when free of teaching commitments. She bore her illness with great fortitude, but it was sad to see her during the final six months gradually getting thinner and less coherent as the painkillers took control. June 25th 1982 had been their Golden Wedding Anniversary and we had celebrated with a special dinner in Usk. Now two and half years later, the person who I loved above all others was no more. It took me at least a year to recover from her death. I still have the photo, taken by a neighbour, of Dad, Mother, Chris and I in the garden at Usk, the garden which was her pride and joy, on the occasion of their fiftieth wedding anniversary. It hangs in a prominent position, as does her portrait, to remind me how much I owe to her love and guidance.

Our final holiday together in August 1986 was at my brother's villa in Callosa, Spain with ready access to the beaches of the Costa Blanca and nearby beauty spots at the castle of Guadalest and Falls of Algar. It was idyllic, though less so for Denise, who catered for our needs back at the house,when the locals were at siesta. The children slept in bunk beds, though Elise caused our concern when she fell from the top bunk onto the hard floor. I swept her up in my arms and carried her downstairs, a moment neither of us has forgotten. Our summer holidays in 1987 took us to Canada where I began to realise all was not well with our marriage. Denise spent time with her family in Montreal, whilst the children and I stayed with my friend John Jones and his wife and children at his cottage on Trouser Lake near Eastman in the Eastern Townships. Halfway through the long holiday Denise took the children to Montreal and I stayed with my cousin Maureen in Ottawa.When the children joined their mother in Montreal I was able to do some serious marathon training, which resulted in a personal best in the Glasgow marathon on our return. Later the children rejoined me at Maureen and her husband Alan's cottage at Sharbot Lake, Ontario. Alan had built the cottage and we had a lot of fun canoeing and wind surfing on the lake. On our return to Britain Denise said she wanted a divorce on the grounds of incompatibility.

Looking back on my divorce it can now be seen as for the best, though I often wonder and hope it had no long term effect on James and Elise. It had come to a head after twelve years together. I think it began for me when Denise was in hospital for a week or so and felt I was not showing sufficient concern or love towards her. I visited with both children but suspect that my concern to 'mother' then led to neglect in my attitude to her at a time when she most needed me to show my affection. This had always been a stumbling block in our relationship. Sex was a rare event and this was the rock on which we floundered. Later a marriage counsellor tried to take me back to my early roots, school days and parental intimacies. This seemed to be leading nowhere as I had no respect for the counsellor who seemed to only see my wife's side of things. In retrospect I suppose I based our relationship on that of my father and mother, which lacked outward signs of their love for each other. To this day the present trend, especially amongst the young, for hugging and kissing, outward signs of emotion, I find overdone, though I go along with it when required. French Canadians, to generalise unforgivably, are a tactile people, not afraid of showing outward emotion; the English are the reverse. Denise was shown more sympathy by the neighbour with whom she shared many cups of coffee and her hospital psychologist, than by me regrettably. I resented being called upon to mind the children on arriving home after a stressful day's teaching. My running training from out of the house also seemed to cause her more concern than when I played rugby and was absent for most of a Saturday afternoon and evening, arriving home the worse for wear. My subsidised trips abroad to Russia and then Japan also caused resentment as she was left to look after the children for some weeks on her own. The grounds of incompatibility my lawyer said was the weakest petition he had ever seen. However I had no chance of obtaining custody over our children unless my wife was a drug addict or prostitute! The law in this respect is an ass, though I gather some attempt has been, and is being made, to redress the balance which sees many men denied access to their children, which is not good for either. As it was, the children suffered, especially Elise, whose sleep was affected. She was only seven at the time.

There followed a rotten six months in which I was consigned to sleeping in the living room before the divorce went through and I moved to Potters Bar from our home in East Barnet. My father tried hard to keep us together, but to no avail. Denise's mind was made up. In retrospect it was probably for the best, as our personalities and interests were very different and neither of us would accommodate to the other sufficiently. With the divorce still very much in the front of my mind I went with staff from Highgate Wood School on a ski holiday to Courchevel in the half term holiday of February 1988.

Denise found a soulmate in Michael Newman, another Art teacher. We sold Brookside South eventually and they moved to Southgate and took out a mortgage on a larger property where they lived with our children and their daughter Pascale before moving eventually to Canada. Our divorce as divorces go was relatively amicable and we still have our children's interests in common. It was good to see Denise and Michael at Elise and James' weddings, and both our children are very fond of Pascale and she of them. Elise visits her mother fairly frequently and James occasionally. Rumour has it that our grandchildren may be the lure to bring them one day back to this country. I hope so.

There were few restrictions to my access to our children, though I was concerned that Denise might decide one day to return to Canada with them. We agreed that I should look after them on alternate weekends and for half of their school holidays. For the next two years the children and I went to the Channel Islands for part of our summer holidays. On Jersey we stayed in a hotel near St Helier on St Aubin's Bay. They went to Jersey Zoo, a butterfly farm and enjoyed the swimming pool and beaches. On Guernsey we stayed at the delightful Saints Bay hotel, walked the cliff path to Petit Port beach below, and even had drinks at the tea garden at Moulin Huet favoured by my mother. I took them in our hired little red Ford Fiesta to all those places I remembered from my childhood. In between these two holidays they climbed Sugar Loaf Mountain above Abergavenny in Gwent, when staying with my father.

By now, entering the final decade of the 20th century, I was living not far from the children in East Barnet and the school in Hornsey. James, not Jamie any more, and Elise were aged thirteen and eleven, both at secondary school. As well as holidays abroad I took every opportunity to visit my father living alone now in Usk and my Aunt Elaine in Bexhill-on-Sea in Sussex. The children enjoyed the change from London suburbia. In London we all visited my brother's exhibition on a corner of Hyde Park, of camel culture, with the unusual sight of camels outside the confines of the zoo.

Christmas 1994 saw me catering for the children on the festive day. Skiing, marathon running and trips with the children to Spain and the Channel Islands became the way of the single man. It was always a doomsday scenario that Denise would take them permanently to Canada. This never happened.

Chapter 13

FINAL YEARS TEACHING, RETIREMENT AND THEREAFTER

After our divorce was completed in 1988, I moved to a one bedroom ground floor apartment of a house in Highview Close, Potters Bar, Hertfordshire. Here I lived from 1988 until 1997. Above me lived an elderly lady who was hard of hearing, so that I had the dubious pleasure of hearing her TV as well as my own. I had a small patch of front and back garden, separate kitchen and lounge/ dining room. My interest in gardening continued to develop slowly in the circumstances. I motored into work at Highgate Wood School each weekday. The journey took roughly half an hour and involved a section climbing through the open ground around Alexandra Palace and then dropping down to Hornsey.

Recreation time revolved around road running, cricket, watching rugby and making fixtures as Fixture Secretary for Haringey RFC. Often I took James and Elise to our cricket in Enfield Park on Sunday afternoons. I looked after their welfare on alternate weekends and for half of every longer holiday. It was quite a squeeze in my one bedroom apartment when they stayed. During the longer holidays I took them to the Channel Islands, Greece, Crete and to my brothers villa in Spain. I was much absorbed during these years in my work as Head of History Department, Schools Exam Officer, Form Tutor and Deputy Head of the Arts Faculty.

Certain incidents may be worth recounting. One Christmas it was my turn to look after our children. I had never had to cater for myself, let alone two children, during the festive season. Fortunately Marks and Spencer's food emporium came to my rescue. Christmas at home as a boy wasn't Christmas without bread sauce as a complement to the turkey. I remember having difficulty in making the bread sauce and realising, rather late in life, how much went in to organising a successful Christmas experience.

Cricket with the Haringey RFC cricket section merits a couple of paragraphs. I used to keep wicket and much enjoyed taking the fast bowling as the ball thumped into the gloves, though I never mastered the technique of standing up to the spinners. Considered a batsmen, bereft of the drive, I accumulated mainly by paddling to leg, and forward defensive pushes. Geoffrey Boycott was quicksilver compared to my rate of scoring. We once won a cup at Bury St Edmunds. The circumstances were interesting. It involved a three way tournament between the local club, Sunderland FC supporters and ourselves, the latter both up from London by train. We began by drinking four pints of ale in reputably the smallest pub in England in Bury. Amazingly this preparation seemed to improve my wicket keeping! Mike Pearce, who had a senior position on the "Hornsey Journal" newspaper, and I were left at the wicket with runs to make and overs, limited to twenty, running out. Our stand, in which I contributed twenty-nine, won the game and ultimately we returned to London clutching the trophy. The whole weekend was reminiscent of the immortal story of the village cricket match as told by A.G. Macdonell in "England their England", Chapter VII. His village cricket field was perfect, though it did lack Bury's oak tree on the field of play.

The concentration required to keep wicket, if only for twenty overs, often gave me a headache. In the end I had to give way to another enthusiast on the grounds of my age. It was never quite the same fielding at fine leg or third man as I found the distance to the wicket often defeated my attempts to throw the ball in on the full, and ended in someone having to back up the throw. This was embarrassing. However, on one occasion I was pleased to be fielding in the deep at long on. It was August bank holiday in 1991 and the club were on tour to Shrewsbury. Our second match at Welshpool saw a Montgomeryshire county player compile a century against us. Immediately after reaching his hundred he opened his shoulders and hit the ball like a bullet at waist height straight at me. Through sheer self-preservation I stood my ground and clung on. Congratulations rained upon me. I hardly dared explain that I couldn't have got out of the way had I wanted to. My cricket career came to an ignominious end in 1995 when I ended a bad patch of batting for the Highgate Wood staff team by being awarded a fine looking trophy for the 'Worse Batting' for that season! Thenceforth I would stick to running.

As for my working life, I have already explained how this ended in 1996 with a stress related depression at the end of the winter term in 1995, after which I only returned for my official leaving in 1996. The illness was brought on by the head teacher's desire to save money by computerising the school's external examination entries. For twelve years I had done this with never an error by entering pupils' longhand, a laborious but proven process. Now I was given half a day's computer training, with the deputy head leering at my ineptitude. I realised I should have to devolve the entry system henceforth between Haringey Council, the school secretary, Margaret Grimes, and myself. Things began to go wrong and a small group of pupils were mistakenly entered for the wrong exam in German. The consequences were not dire, but the local press got hold of the story. This preyed on my mind in the following year, when an Ofsted school inspection was due. Could something similar happen again? Would the wrath of Chris Woodhead, H.M Inspector General, descend on me and ruin my career. I began falling asleep immediately upon getting home after work, a sure sign of mental exhaustion. Anyway, the anxiety depression occurred. I was prescribed Prozac which made the condition worse and my usual doctor avoided me. Finally, having seen various practitioners, I arrived at Dr Caroline Dain who bothered to look up my symptoms and recommend the right anti-depressive to treat them. I began to build back my self confidence in early retirement. Fulfilment through success in running and starting to teach History again at Enfield's University of the Third Age, assisted this process. On Valentine's Day, for a year or two thereafter, I presented Dr Dain with a rose as a token of my thanks.

In October 1996 I took my first lesson with the History group at U3A. We met in one of the group's apartments. The group numbered nine persons, were very enthusiastic and kept me on my toes. The history of London from Prehistoric to Modern Times was the topic I chose, as in thirty-six years a teacher I had never been expected to teach my own city's past. Nineteen years later there are still some members of that first class, in what became my Monday group. They include the indispensable Toni Borthwick, in charge of money and refreshments, and the sister, Lyn Harrison, of June Weston, in whose flat we first met.

Dr Caroline Dain suggested plenty of outside interests to counteract depression. I decided it was time to begin my retirement years in a new house, free from old memories. It's now nearly nineteen years since I moved into my present house. I had spent some months before house hunting in rural Hertfordshire. The delightful villages of Essendon, Bayford and Brickendon were fine in summer, but seemed rather isolated and lonely in winter. St Albans, though historic, was too large. The Bengeo side of Hertford had my house, but it was set aside, it transpired, for a relative. Another suitable dwelling in Brookmans Park had a sort of yellowish tide mark around the walls and still smelt of smoke. I just wasn't in luck until I visited 6 Inglefield, on the polite side of Potters Bar known as Little Heath. An ex–policeman, Jim Read, who wanted to move south of the river showed me over and I "found it much to my liking", my diary records.

As soon as I walked in I felt at home and first impressions were reinforced when I noticed it was well maintained; in all of close on twenty years, I hesitate to admit, I have only ever decorated two of the half dozen rooms. The views over the surrounding area and the potential of the garden seemed considerable. Moreover it was a quiet retreat in a close, comprising eight houses, "in sought after cul-de-sac location". The extended through lounge/dining room with a serving hatch to the kitchen was spatially palatial after my bachelor pad on the wrong side of Potters Bar. This had become cramped and depressing in retirement, especially when I had to accommodate my children in the single bedroom.

I had found the house I wanted. Now a buyer for my maisonette materialised in the shape of Brian Mason, a member of my University of the Third Age History class. Brian wanted to move into smaller accommodation and was happy to accept an offer for some of his furniture, including a large sofa. Moving day arrived and began tragically as my friend Tony Spinks had a mild heart attack while attempting to move said sofa. I remember doing a U-turn on the North Circular to get him to Emergency at the North Middlesex hospital, where after an ECG he was diagnosed. I felt responsible in part and phoned his wife before continuing until 10 pm, finally moving in the washing machine with the help of my son. I went to bed exhausted at 2am, and vowed that if ever I move again I shall employ professionals!

As I look out of my window while writing this I realise that I made the right decision. Mountgrace school at the back means that on a fine day I still hear the sounds of school children at play and from upper windows can see their games of rounders, rugby or football. It reminds me of my thirty-six year career as a teacher at a similar comprehensive secondary school, albeit mainly in History, but with some Games. The seven neighbourly homes in the close have seen some comings and goings, but two are unchanged in ownership. All are good friends. It is a good location, within walking distance of shops and railway station, twenty minutes by train to the world's grandest city. Yet it is in the so-called Green Belt with playing fields to the rear, enabling me to spot some forty-seven avian varieties from herons, pheasants and recently flocks of parrots to the green woodpecker who digs for ants on my lawns. The only query that has exercised me over the years is why did Jim Read install indoor locks and have a klaxon–sounding burglar alarm? As an ex-policeman was he afraid of some criminal exacting retribution? For me, I have always felt both safe and snug in my home, with visitors, my children or alone.

The years of retirement have been based on and about my home first and foremost. I have endeavoured to improve the property in some way in most of the last twenty years. The garden has been a source of interest and recreation for much of each year. The small pond attracts frogs and frogs spawn each spring. The year begins with the snowdrops, crocus and narcissus. The dogwood's branches add a touch of midwinter fire to the prevailing white, purple and yellow. Early spring heralds the white blossoms of *Amelanchier ballerina*, a medium sized tree. April brings the deep pinkish-red of the flowering currant in the front garden and tulips everywhere. Fritillaries hang bell-like with their lovely shape and chequered pattern. Around the pond the primulas, and in the pond the yellow caltha join the ball. In the rockery, aptly named rock roses and saxifrage push aside the encroaching ivy. By May and June the cornflowers and lupin are blooming. High summer in July sees my arch fragrant with climbing jasmine and pink roses. The flowering winter pansies and violas in the hanging baskets give way to petunia, begonia and fuchias. So the days begin to shorten and autumn arrives with the exotic Dahlia 'pasodoble', and the unfortunately named but equally exotic Dahlia 'pooh'. A spread of Japanese anemones in the front, kaffir lilies, orange and red crocosmia in the back, and the final water lilies in the pond end the flowering season as we enter winter again. Here the winter jasmine and hellebores continue to defy nature, as do the conifers secluding my garden from the world beyond.

In addition to my growing passion for gardening, an interest in history beyond my career has led to a role in the local history society of Potters Bar and District. For many years it has been my job to hire a wide variety of speakers, one each month from September to May, to inform and enliven society members on historical topics pertaining to our Hertfordshire locality. Looking through past records we have had the adventures of an Edwardian lady parachutist, the history of Elstree film studios over the last hundred years, and the intriguing tale of the Great Bed of Ware. Follow-up visits are sometimes made; a walk along the River Stort perhaps or a visit to

Cromer, the last windmill in Hertfordshire.

Because of other commitments such as writing this autobiography, it has been necessary to cut down on private tuition in history. Advanced level tuition is especially challenging. Recently the parents of a bright young Asian girl, Rohini, living in Hemel Hempstead, asked whether I could help clear a mental block she had in relating to the history of the Norman Conquest. It was not a part of history that I knew enough about to enlighten an A-level student, so we learned together, and from a projected C/D Grade she improved to an A*, enabling her to enter London School of Economics. Earlier I had offered English and had many similar worthwhile rewarding experiences, though it sometimes meant reading an unread novel like "Wuthering Heights" and analysing it within a few days at Advanced level. This was an experience which I found very demanding, so latterly I only offered History, where the necessary research was more attainable.

University of the Third Age, Enfield branch, has become very much a part of retirement for nearly two decades. My Monday class began in 1996, mushroomed into a Tuesday morning group which began a year later. They meet in alternate weeks and have had a number of venues. At present we are located in a room at the back of St Paul's Hall, Enfield, which accommodates just over twenty people. Since both groups have twenty-five or more, we are at present full. I try to encourage discussion and active participation. The emphasis in Monday's group is on a chronology of British history. Tuesday's group choose their own topics, which have ranged from the American West to Ancient Egypt, from the History of London to that of Scotland. Monday's group continue the habit of visits into London. In recent times the ceremony of the keys at the Tower of London, Wilton's Variety Theatre in the East End, Kensington Palace and the Dickens Museum have been patronised.

Being within half an hour of London by train and underground has meant that my visits are frequent, especially to the West End theatre through U3A's group matinees organised by Barbara Saunders. Also the Enfield U3A's Photographic group, organised by Sara Davis once a month, arranges excursions to all sorts of places in the metropolis and beyond deemed to have photographic potential. The World Wildlife Photographer of the Year exhibition at the Natural History Museum is a regular date.

Another regular date in my retirement is with Trent Park Running Club's training weekend, less for the training than for the opportunity of experiencing places further afield. In 2015 we met at Stoke Rochford Hall, a fine Victorian pile in Lincolnshire. Exploring Grantham, a small town which had seen better times when on the A1 to the North, I also took the opportunity to visit Woodsthorpe Manor, birthplace of Isaac Newton. The apple tree in the garden purports to be the very one which led him to devise the theory of gravity. It was suitably gnarled and twisted to be that old.

Finally mention must be made of the RSPB (Royal Society for the Protection of Birds) whose local meetings take place conveniently in a church hall a short walk from my home. They have interesting speakers with collections of photographs of unbelievable beauty from all quarters of the globe. Coach trips are run to stately homes and gardens. Recently, as recounted, I fulfilled a long held wish to see eagles in the Pyrenees with them, and shortly will travel to Morocco with my brother and nine others to explore that country's various birdlife. They also have quizzes and I do enjoy a good quiz. A member of my U3A History class, Pat Large, organises a group and we display our knowledge, or lack of it, at a variety of local venues. Nowadays we win rarely, perhaps a sign of advancing years, but it remains an enjoyable social occasion.

To complete the picture of a full, vigorous and challenging retirement agenda, I need to cover my global travelling. That will take another volume, which I promise to write if this is sufficiently popular. Meantime you need to appreciate how essential my family is to my happiness at present and this will be the subject of my final chapters.

Chapter 14

MY AFRICAN FAMILY

My brother, Chris, has lived most of his adult life in East Africa, first of all in Uganda and then in Kenya. My first experience of Africa came in 1963 when, aged twenty-seven, I visited him in Kampala and the Queen Elizabeth National Park, Uganda. Flying via Rome, I was met at Nairobi by Dick Ling, our erstwhile neighbour in Woodford Essex, then farming in Kenya. On the way to his sumptuous bungalow in the foothills of Mount Elgon at Kitale in Kenya we stopped to admire the views over the Rift Valley, and later Lake Nakuru. I was "blown away" by the sheer scale of the scenery. In the next few days Dick introduced me to the life of a British farmer in Kenya, another unique experience. Kenya was recently independent and he was having to adjust to post-colonial life under Jomo Kenyatta. Later he was to move on to Australia and now lives in semi-retirement, still in touch with the land and sheep, in Devon.

Chris picked me up in Kitale, and we drove to Kampala, where we stayed overnight at Makerere University. Next day he took me in his Austin A40 to Kilembe, a copper mining town, not far from the Q.E. Park. Driving on the murram dirt roads required a special technique to avoid pot holes and ridges of dirt which could rot a car. On arrival at the headquarters of the Queen Elizabeth Park at Mweya, there began a series of exciting events. A launch trip along the Kazinga Channel, separating Lake Edward from Lake George, introduced me to hippo, buffalo and elephant aplenty. Chris was involved in a project which meant culling hippo. The hippo were shot and their meat sold to the locals. At Ishasha camp in the park the lion spend part of their day in the trees, which is quite unusual. We spent the night sleeping in an open *banda* (hut) under mosquito nets with lion in the vicinity. Chris assured me that as long as I stayed within my net, the lion would not bother me. To me this was scarcely reassuring and I slept very little that night. During the next few weeks I got used to eating hippo, buffalo and even lion and cane rat.

One especially rewarding trip was via Fort Portal to the hot springs and forest behind the Ruwenzori range, known as the Mountains of the Moon. There we met pigmy tribespeople. On another occasion Chris's colleague, Gerald Clough, took me north to Murchison Falls Park where the Nile crashes spectacularly through gaps in the rainforest. With the Park Warden, John Savidge, we searched for rhino in the bush and rode on the tame white rhino, Obongi, in semi-captivity. Chris and I played rugby for Kilembe and helped the local side win the Uganda cup. Away games involved a weekend well away because of the distances involved. Kilembe's team had a decided Welsh flavour as some of the copper mine personnel were ex-South Wales' coal miners.

I didn't return to Africa again for over thirty years. Much had happened in my brother's and my personal lives. Chris's first marriage had come apart, and he had spent many years in the relative solitude of Mount Kulal in the far north of Kenya working for UNESCO and later for an Anglo-Canadian organisation, Farm Africa. In the remoteness of the Jade sea or Lake Rudolf, as it was then called, his neighbours on the mountain were American missionaries. His work involved contact with the nomadic tribespeople of this vast area where he tried to assist in their way of life based on the camel, rather than on cattle which could not survive drought and desert. Desert encroachment in this void area was becoming a serious environmental concern. Farm Africa had considerable success in spreading their ideas and converting pastoralists. Chris's life's work had been devoted to promoting wildlife and the camel. In 2005 he was to write a book called "Where there is no Development Agency", a manual for pastoralists and their promoters with special reference to the arid regions of the greater Horn of Africa. His ability to pilot Farm Africa's light plane helped him to cover the considerable distances involved in co-ordinating his field work with headquarters in Nanyuki and also with Nairobi.

On December 16th 1995 Chris married again, this time to Nasra Omar, third daughter of Kenyan parents but with origins in Yemen and Somalia. They met at a British army function in the town of Nanyuki, about two hundred kilometres north of Nairobi in the foothills of Mount Kenya. In the spring of 1996 they returned to Britain for a blessing ceremony in South Wales, which my father and their British friends were able to attend. My teenage children and I enjoyed the ceremony at Usk Baptist church and the subsequent reception in Crickhowell.

Chris and Nasra established themselves in Nanyuki and when I visited them in 1997 they had built a beautiful house at the coast, designed by Chris and an Italian builder. The house overlooked the Shimba Hills National Park so that elephant, waterbuck, baboons and buffalo came out of the bush literally at the bottom of the garden. Sable antelope were a common sight on the hillside further away, being a rare, more timid, very beautiful creature. Chris named his house at the coast appropriately "Sable Fields". From the house, a journey down a road studded with potholes, taking around half an hour, brought you to Ukunda and nearby glorious tropical coral sand beaches at Diani. Diani is but a short distance by road and ferry from Mombasa, where Fort Jesus and the narrow streets and hand-carved wooden doors of the old town are reminders of its Arab and Portuguese past. A snorkelling trip by dhow to an offshore marine national park revealed multi-coloured tropical fish and extensive coral. We visited Nasra's family and met her parents and numerous brothers and sisters. Two of Chris's young nephews came with us to the Bamburi Nature Reserve and enjoyed giant tortoise and hippo close-up.

Back in Nanyuki we motored and hiked to the old Moses Hut at 11,500 feet on Mount Kenya whose magnificent scenery, giant lobelia and sunbirds gave me a desire to return again one day. Finally I was given a taste of the empty north of Kenya, when we travelled to Maralal to visit a camel butchery opened by Chris, as project leader of Farm Africa. On this safari we reached an eminence at Poror where the full extent of the Rift Valley could be viewed from a vantage point. Later I had to join three photos to give the view its full visual impact. The framed photograph decorates my lounge now with my brother and two Kenyan children framing what is, to my mind, an incomparable natural vista. Before returning to the United Kingdom I was able to get a haircut at Nasra's new salon which she opened alongside her restaurant, called "CamCorner" in Nanyuki at this time.

On New Year's Eve 1998 I found myself on an Emirates flight to Dubai in transit for Nairobi. Not a lot stirred there during a very brief visit, as it was Ramadhan. Chris and Nasra were waiting at Nairobi airport, having left my niece Anita, born on April 6th 1998, in the care of Nasra's younger sister Zahra. April 6th coincidentally was also my brother's birthday, so he became a father when fifty-eight precisely. At Muthaiga Club I met my niece for the first time. The club retains the atmosphere of pre-independent colonial India. Members must dress appropriately for dinner. Dessert is presented on a multi-tiered trolley full of tempting trifles, sundaes and layered cakes. The staff assume suitably subservient attitudes. A stuffed lion in the corridor is as old as my father, then ninety-three. The club has a comforting atmosphere totally divorced from the hurly-burly of the real world of contemporary Nairobi. A walk around the golf course is delightful with colourful butterflies, gorgeous blossoms, kites and ibis and that commodity lacking in a British winter, a warm tropical sun. It is made all the more comforting by being able to hear the chaotic cacophony on a nearby roundabout, but without being part of it.

Both of Kenya's main cities, Nairobi and Mombasa, are overpopulated and security, especially for the single European at night-time, is an ever present issue. In Nanyuki, well north of Nairobi, and at the coast it was more relaxing, though beggars at one and beach boys at the other could still be a nuisance. To escape completely you needed to travel to the far north, or to the renowned game parks or beyond, losing oneself in the national wonders of East Africa. This I was able to do with Chris as a guide and Nasra an ever-willing hostess. East Africa is probably the best area for bird watching in the world. Its savannah grasslands, tropical scrub and thorn forest is ideal habitat for ornithologists. In a matter of a few weeks on this visit I recorded over one hundred species. Breakfast was accompanied by weaver birds at Lake Baringo and we moved on to Lake Bogoria where there were some four million flamingos.

The cultural differences always made visits to Chris's African family interesting. Nasra is a Moslem and Chris also follows some practices of that faith. In those days he fasted during Ramadhan, and when that discipline ended, the feast that followed at Eid was something special. A sheep was slaughtered and those invited tore into great hunks of mutton on the bone and rice, right hands working overtime! The chewing of *miraa* or *khat*, a stimulant now banned in England, kept people chatting noisily far into the night.

The journey from Nairobi to the coast at Mombasa by road was a national disgrace, especially after the rains when there were long sections of detoured unmade roads and other rough and potholed lengths. After this experience of some six hours, the Sable Field's house and Diani beach's white sands made it all worthwhile. Sometimes we rented a beach house for a day or two with views through palm trees to the reef beyond, with surf breaking over it. Nas had a somewhat perverse sense of humour and gave me a scare when she put a very realistic mock snake under my seat at the dinner table. She also got me using the gym, when going into hysterics at my feeble efforts to clamber aboard a boat we had hired, to view the wonders of the deep.

I take the opportunity during most of my visits to my brother's family in Africa to travel to another part of that continent. In 1999 I spent ten days in Zanzibar, but that and later journeys to Ethiopia,

Botswana, Namibia and Zambia will feature in what may be a sequel to this autobiography describing my experiences travelling beyond Europe.

On my return from Zanzibar, Chris, a German friend, Heinz Muller, and I flew north in the Farm Africa Cessna to Ngurunit. The airstrip was seldom used and we were welcomed by an old man, his son and numerous children who emerged to see the unusual sight. We were in the seldom visited arid lands of northern Kenya, to see a water catchment scheme which Farm Africa had constructed to provide surface water for the tribes-people of the area. Next day we walked steadily for four and a half hours, with a brief break in great heat, until reaching the final watering hole where Samburu herds-men were attending a herd of camels. We then had a long break, and finally camped after another two hours walking up a sand river, in the early evening. Our goods and chattels were carried by camels, which also carried our water. The next two or three days of our camel safari followed a similar pattern. Wambile, a tribal elder, his wife, and a young man, Francis, were our guides. At one point Francis climbed down steeply to replenish our water from an underground source. We used that water for washing. One of the camels took some time to retrieve, when it bolted, shedding its load of water and camping equipment. The heat was excessive and oasis in the bush and semi-desert were welcome rest stops in the hottest hours. By the penultimate day I had developed blisters on both feet and felt utterly exhausted. Mission accomplished, the catchment area photographed and noted, I was only too glad to see our plane on the final day. We had slept under the stars with the grunts of lion in the distance, our camels tethered nearby.

From the experience, I learnt I was no Bear Grylls. The camel was wonderfully adapted to the environment with its steady walking pace and large padded feet. Finally, water, which we take so for granted, is life and death in that sort of environment. We had trekked fifty or more miles and it was equivalent to running a marathon and a half in energy expanded, but an enlightening experience.

Life in Nanyuki at the time revolved around Chris's camels, Nasra's hair salon and baby Anita with an elderly maidservant, Mary, acting as nurse, cook and laundry maid. Mary was invaluable and it was fitting that I was able to contribute something towards her son Patrick's education. He kept me informed of his progress in the following years and has done well. Unemployment is at a very high level in Kenya. The menagerie of cats, guard dogs, geese and rabbits at and around the house coupled security with companionship for the children, for Nasra was now pregnant with Leila, their second daughter.

By this time a fairly prolonged visit to Kenya lasting from early December to early February had become customary. Leila, born in October 1999, was just over a year old when I visited again. In the middle of January 2001 I started dating Winnie Alila, who was working as Chris's secretary at the time. Although we were a generation apart in age this seemed not to matter.

It was however with another Winnie and Josphat as mountain guides that Chris and I spent five days on Mount Kenya during this visit. By the third day we were in Shipton's Hut below Point Lenana, third highest peak on the mountain and inaccessible without roped climbing experience. That day a party had returned because of the icy conditions, so when we set out at 3am with torches to light our way up the 4,600 metre peak, we were apprehensive. Some of the near vertical snow slopes were frightening, and we were pleased when another group equipped with ice axes joined us. They helped cut steps we could use and by 6am we had struggled to the top, where our efforts were rewarded by the sunrise over the magnificent mountain scenery. Later that day we took on the endless swamp, myself in boots which leaked, and arrived at the base hut, having covered 25 kilometres. One of our party, who had climbed in North Wales, said that our climb had been category one and as such, with our lack of equipment, quite risky.

New Year 2002 was an occasion to remember. Most New Years are disappointing. After an excellent meal overlooking the Indian

Ocean, Winnie, Nasra and Anita and Leila, Chris and I watched a
firework display further up the beach under a full moon on the coral
sand. It was the sort of romantic setting that dreams are made of.
After dancing at the local disco, we disturbed nightjar and bush pig
on the way home to "Sable Fields" in the hills in the early hours of
New Year's Day.

Our climb of Point Lenana on Mount Kenya had given Chris and
I the idea of attempting the high level circular route. This took five
days and involved some hard and lengthy climbing at altitude. The
glorious mountain scenery made the effort very worthwhile. The
third day culminated with a lung sapping hour and a half climb to
Austrian Hut at 15,720 feet. We slept on hard foam mattresses briefly,
and from our upper bunk had to practice gymnastic contortions to
exit the squalid hut in the night for toilet purposes in the snow. The
scenic Chogoria route off the mountain remains immortalised in
my hall today with a photo of the precipitous edge of the Gorges
canyon framed in bamboo from off the mountain. An incident with
an elephant and the near loss of my camera down a toilet long drop
sealed what were five days full of impact. My two expeditions of
Mount Kenya had been memorable. Mount Kilimanjaro, highest in
Africa, now beckoned.

In January 2003, with Henry Morrison, a Scottish running friend,
we were on the shuttle bus for Tanzania from Nairobi, bound for the
town of Moshi and Kilimanjaro. Next morning we awoke at 5am to
the wail of the muezzin calling the faithful to prayer. The porters got
their loads weighed and we went through registration procedures.
I noticed that aged sixty-seven at the time, I was one of the oldest
attempting the climb, though somewhat reassured when informed
that an eighty year old had succeeded sometime in the past. Nuru,
a young porter, carrying twenty-five kilograms on his back, led the
way up the path. Freddie, our guide, had earlier come to Kenya
to become acquainted. He was Tanzanian, as Josphat our Kenyan
guide was not allowed to lead parties on Kilimanjaro, a Tanzanian
preserve.

The first two days involved little more than a hard day's walking, through rainforest followed by moorland, for around five to six hours, with a break for lunch. We were following the standard route to the summit, and in the evening of the first day we had a scenic walk to acclimatise. Leaving Mandara camp on the second day, we gained one thousand metres (three thousand three hundred feet) through giant lobelia and groundsel, with views of the snow-capped Kibo summit and the nearby dramatic Mawenzi Mountain. Day two took us up to Horombo where we arrived after five and half hours and where we should have acclimatised for another day. To save money we didn't do this and were to pay the price. The third day took us past the last drinking point. Two litres per person a day would now need carriage. Crossing the high Alpine desert, wind-swept and bare at altitude, now took us to Kibo, the final hut, before the climb that night up the steep scree slope to Gilman's Point, on the rim of the crater. Henry was suffering from tummy trouble, so it was Freddie and I who set out at around 1am in the pitch black early next morning to climb the scree to Gilman's at 5,680 (18,744). The ultimate day is rather more than a walk at altitude, as had been suggested by a well-wisher on our bus journey to Moshi.

Other groups could be traced from the twinkling lights of their head torches above, winding back and forth across the mountain, gaining height with every traverse. It was an almost subconscious dream-like scene. Beyond Hans Meyer cave at about 5,000 metres (16,500 feet) Freddie insisted I drink a whole litre of water and we pressed on, passing other groups, into an area of large boulders near the top. I began to feel dizzy and had a bout of altitude sickness.

The final twenty minutes were done five minutes at a time, until reaching Gilman's, magically just before sunrise. The scenery was worth the considerable pain, looking down into the volcanic crater, the ice fields and across to Mawenzi, now below us with the sun rising behind it. It had taken six hours, and I declined to go round the crater rim to Uhuru Point at 5,896 metres (19,457 feet), margin-ally higher, on Freddie's orders. I regret it to this day, though in returning I did get the certificate saying that a height of 5,680 metres (18,744 feet) had been reached. We came down in just two hours to Kibo, where we re-joined Henry, myself using the words of Steve Redgrave, "If anyone asks me to do that again, you have my permission to shoot me". Returning to Horombo, I had been walking for eleven hours. Further paths down next day resulted in very sore feet, a state of total exhaustion but great contentment.

By now a number of factors were leading me toward East Africa every December for Christmas and New Year, with the air fare most reasonable well before Christmas and well after New Year. My African family which now included Winnie, the contrast between British and Kenyan weather at that time of year, and a trip to some exotic African location beyond Kenya, were reasons enough for my annual migration.

In 2004-2005 Chris and I had a very interesting tour around the historic origins of Ethiopia with a memorable detour into the Simien Mountains. James and Elise joined us in the last days of 2004 for their first experience of Africa or any developing country. Their reactions were interesting. They found it hard to come to terms with the master-servant relationship which exists in parts of the white community, whether indigenous or foreign. They certainly packed a wide variety of new experiences into their two weeks stay, from camel riding to snorkelling off a dhow. Temporarily they lost their way, Elise her wallet, and both learnt the technique of bargaining. All in all they returned to England more mature and better informed than when they left.

The topic of malaria arose when time was spent at the coast and as I took precautions I always remained unaffected. On my trip in 2006-07 however I suffered from what was diagnosed by Chris's doctor as a secondary infection. This was picked up possibly at the airport or on a delayed flight to the coast and lasted for all of my stay. Nasra's oldest sister, Zenab, passed away in January 2007. Moslem funerals take place within twenty-four hours and are followed by three days of mourning. This was also the last time I saw Winnie, so it was a less than happy vacation on that occasion.

After a gap of two years, when I next visited, Chris drove me to the Karen suburb of Nairobi, where the house had a very pleasant fifty metre garden and twenty-five metre pool. Anita, now eleven years old, was like her father, a very good swimmer. This was encouraged at Braeburn school where the girls had an American coach. The school followed the English model in secondary education and both my nieces seemed very happy there. This time my stay was enlivened by the presence of my cousin Maureen's daughter, Andrea, husband Dennis and children Jayden and Kaelyn. They had arrived from Vancouver and with them I spent a memorable safari in the Masai Mara game park. Serena Lodge, where we stayed over the New Year of 2010, looked out over the vast expanse of the Mara and game drives were scheduled every morning and afternoon. The variety of game and birdlife was outstanding. Especially so was a female cheetah with three cubs. My new digital camera worked overtime taking sixty photos of this family alone. One morning we breakfasted by the crossing point used by the herds of wildebeest and zebra on their annual migration in search of fresher grazing, beset by hungry crocodile.

Anita had participated in the sub-Saharan swimming championships held in Nairobi in January 2010 and in December later that year we accompanied her to South Africa for a training camp. Christmas was spent at a desirable residence overlooking Table Mountain in Cape Town. The sun setting behind the mountain left an enduring memory. The beaches were warm, but windy where the great ocean currents met. Parasailing was very popular. Memories linger of days of wine and roses that winter in Cape Town. The Kirstenbosch botanical gardens bloomed with exotic flowers such as the pincushion proteas, darling hyacinth and bird of paradise flower. Christmas day lunch consisted of a superb fish platter at an open air restaurant on the waterfront. Here the wind was so strong that the menu, serviettes and someone else's drink all ended up in my lap! Chris and I also enjoyed Stellenbosch, where at the Simon-sig winery we relished tasters of different wines supervised by the elegant hostess, Lara von Antwerp! A trip to Robben Island brought us down to earth with a bump as Chris and I relived Mandela's life on the prison island. From Cape Town Chris, Leila and I flew via Johannesburg and Gaborone, capital of Botswana, to Maun, for a few days in the Okavango Delta. Chris remained in Botswana for some months training their camels for tourism.

It was another year before I re-joined my distant family in Africa. Leila had climbed Point Lenana on Mount Kenya. Anita had won a gold, two silver and four bronze medals in the subSaharan swimming championships in Botswana and now was breaking a host of Kenyan national records for her age group. Leila's prowess at hockey and her artistic talent were becoming more evident. On this occasion I took off after Christmas with a cosmopolitan group, all younger, for Windhoek, capital of Namibia. The organisers were Wild Dog Safaris and the others were to camp. Every evening after a meal round the camp fire while they set up their tents, I was taken to a nearby hotel. I was, after all, seventy-six by now and claimed the privilege of age. On the only occasion that a hotel was not accessible, I was provided with a large tent, pitched for me, to myself.

Later, back in Kenya, Chris and I spent an interesting day at Hell's Gate near Naivasha in the Rift Valley. In this national park the scenery and animal life are features, as is the narrow gorge. Not long ago a flash flood caught children on a school journey party unawares. Seven were drowned, being unable to escape up the precipitous sides of the gorge. At the elephant orphanage in Nairobi I adopted a baby elephant. This concern, run by Daphne Sheldrick, wife of a former park warden, nurtures junior elephants orphaned often through poaching for ivory and later releases them back into the wild.

My brother's wife and daughter moved temporarily to England in 2014 so that Anita, who aspired to reach the 2016 Olympics, could receive better coaching. They set up home in Yelverton, Devon, in a fine house overlooking Dartmoor. The girls went to school in

Tavistock at Kelly College. Thus, it was that my most recent visit to Africa was in the company of Steven Smith, owner of the Devon property. When holiday time arrived, Nasra and the girls joined us. We all celebrated Chris and Nasra's nineteenth wedding anniversary. Steven and I tried our hand at milking camels with varying degrees of success and enjoyed a day at the National Museum and at the Railway Museum in Nairobi. Later from "Sable Fields" at the coast we had an unusual day visiting Funzi island, a Moslem village offshore and reached by canoe. The houses were built on a framework of mangrove, coral and mud. Solar panels and mobile phones added an incongruous touch to what was a primitive lifestyle based on the sea and fishing. The women gathered seaweed, sold in the United States for the extraction of perfume. Private European benefactors had sponsored schools and health facilities. A deep well provided the only fresh water. Our lunch consisted of rock lobster, mangrove crab and rock cod in tomato and coconut sauce on rice. It was excellent. We watched the dhows come in with their catches of white snapper while lazing on a pristine sandbank, and then returned to the chaos of urban Africa.

Having read "Out of Africa" by Karen Blixen and seen the film based on the book, starring Robert Redford and Meryl Streep, I was anxious to visit the house. It did not disappoint. The grounds of the house have distant views of the Ngong Hills where she buried her lover Denis Fitch-Hatton after his untimely death in a flying accident. Of more contemporary interest, also in the fringes of Nairobi, was the Kazuri Beads enterprise run by Lady Susan Wood where many women, often single mothers, were employed designing exquisite strings of beads.

Recently Nasra, Anita and Leila have returned to Kenya. I'm sure they missed the warmth, and Leila preferred her school in Kenya. For me their decision to go back is welcome. "Sable Fields" at the coast and "Mahatu pa Migumo" on Nandi Road in Karen, Nairobi, have become a winter's haven of sunshine, beauty and hospitality which I feel very fortunate to be able to enjoy.

Chapter 15

MY OWN FAMILY

In Chapter Ten my early years of marriage were recounted, as well as the happy home life we established with our young children. It will be remembered that one cloud alone marred this bright prospect. Mother had undergone her mastectomy, and she also suffered from rheumatoid arthritis for much of the last ten years of her life. It had been wonderful to see her with Jamie and Elise as young children.

Dad soldiered on for another fifteen years. He was remarkably self-sufficient and resilient. When eighty-six years old he underwent a double heart bypass operation performed by a Sri Lankan surgeon. This was unusual at that time for one of his age. A heart attack when he was sixty had forced him to retire. In retirement he took up yoga and, following the surgeon's advice, took Bovril regularly. The operation cured his angina and gave him another ten good years. His medical history also included a spell hospitalised after an operation on his sciatic nerve, strained when lifting my brother's car on a visit to Africa. His passion was music, chiefly classical. He would listen for hours to his record collection with earphones clamped to his head, strategically placed between the audio amplifiers. The earphones prevented the rest of us and the neighbours hearing the noise, for he was hard of hearing and refused to wear a hearing aid, so the music was unnaturally loud. He believed in pure sound and with a scientific exactitude would tolerate nothing less.

Both he and my mother were products of the pre-Second World War age when times were hard and, because possessions were acquired with difficulty, all the more valued. Their love was expressed in what they did for us, more than in outward show or many gifts. It was an upbringing I feel fortunate to have had.

Mother didn't live to witness my divorce. Jamie and Elise were at a tender age at the time, the former just eleven and Elise eight. Their reactions were quite different. Jamie appeared largely unaffected, whilst Elise's sleep was affected and for a time she was on medication. In retrospect this was to be expected, the one being an introvert, the other more typically extrovert. When checked or thwarted Elise could fly into near uncontrollable tantrums, whilst James was more accepting, superficially anyway.

Dad's ninetieth came and went. Chris and I had organised a special celebration and even had the invitation cards printed, when he changed his mind. He opted for a smaller gathering, which his long-time friend, Mary Mclellan, and her husband Iain hosted in their lovely home overlooking the Monmouthshire countryside, which Dad loved, at Llandenny. Betty Richards, Dad's secretary during his long tenure as manager of Standard Telephones and Cables in Newport, Monmouthshire was there. She entertained my father and I on my frequent visits to South Wales during school holidays, and was famous for her Pavlovas for our dessert. At about this time I acquired a kitten, which we named Twigs after his favourite plaything. Later he took to bringing in anything that moved, from frogs to birds, through the cat flap. One day I came home to find a blackbird causing mayhem trying to escape from the bedroom!

Elise and James both attended Ashmole School in Southgate, North London during their teens; James as a scholar, Elise for gymnastic lessons and displays. She was an excellent gymnast and to see her in one of the displays performing in the various disciplines was a memorable experience. Faced with the choice of a career as a gymnast, with a full time training programme, she decided to continue with it as a social activity, along with riding and later athletics. She went to secondary school at Queen Elizabeth School for Girls in Barnet.

James, as an avid Arsenal supporter, showed promise sufficient to earn a trial as a goalkeeper with Barnet F.C. and had a year between the sticks for Middlesex University. His career path has included a temporary flirtation with sales at prominent outfitters and then an Access course to primary school teaching, and a course in Amenity Horticulture at Capel Manor College, Enfield. He finally settled in the catering profession and thereby met his wife, Clare, who was manager of the Toby Carvery restaurant at Whitewebbs Lane, Enfield. In recent years they have moved to a number of locations within the same franchise, always living on the premises of their place of work. En route from Enfield to Newbury, Berkshire, Weston-super-Mare and finally Clacton-on-Sea, they have acquired a family composing three boys, Hayden, Ellis and Kinley. In Clacton they finally obtained their own house, not far from both beach and pier where they are now more firmly rooted.

Elise, rather like her brother, having taken her A–Levels, tried a number of avenues before settling into an employment niche. She trained as a hairdresser and did a short stint as assistant to an estate agent, before taking a one-way ticket to Canada. Whilst in the Americas she travelled in the United States and in Mexico. Realising that she would have to re-sit her A-Levels if she wanted a career in art and design in Canada, she returned to Britain to study these subjects at Hertfordshire University, doing a Foundation Course. She had found her calling and moved on to London College of Fashion, where she obtained her Degree in Fashion Styling and Photography. Meantime my daughter had met her future husband, Dominic Hall, henceforth known as Dom, at the end of her Foundation year. This convinced her to stay in Britain and they lived in Winchmore Hill, N21, for the next six years. During this period Elise did her work experience at various fashion magazines and landed a position as a fashion assistant on the prestigious magazine Marie Claire.

Dom and Elise were married at the picturesque little church of St Mary's in the Wiltshire village of Alvediston, on July 12th 2008. The reception took place in the great barn at Samways and in a marquee accommodating a hundred guests. My speech was received well and the bride and I danced to "Wind Beneath Your Wings" sung by Bette Midler from the film Beaches, a favourite of mine. The weather behaved and Elise and Dom's family organised everything very effectively. My brother's family came over from Kenya and my cousin Maureen's family joined us from North America, so it was quite a family reunion.

James's wedding to Clare followed on April 29th, 2010 at historic Polhawn Fort, built on the Devon Cornish border overlooking Cawsand Bay. A marquee on the lawn and seventy seats within became the hub of activity for the wedding dinner, speeches and photos. Both my cousins again attended, as did my brother. The weather finally relented for romantic photos taken against the coastal panorama and a magnificent sunset. The decor was a well-chosen white and sea green. Cornish cream tea and Cornish pasties were served, to follow sea bass and Chablis.

Before concluding this autobiography with the arrival and development of my five grandchildren, I should like to bid farewell to the older generation of my family. My father and his sisters, Mavis and Elaine, all became nonagenarians. The oldest, Mavis, died on November 1st 1999 aged ninety-six. She had lived with, and been cared for over many years, by my cousin, Auriol, who had devoted her life to looking after her mother. My father was determined to see in the millennium and achieved his ambition. In December 1999 he had collapsed and been found on the bathroom floor. When I arrived at the Nevill Hall hospital in Abergavenny I found him in bed somewhat confused and suffering bronchitis. After a few days he was discharged but bedridden, so I set up Home Care and an alarm system in case he collapsed again. Christmas day was undoubtedly the most grim I can remember as by now I also was suffering from bronchitis, with paroxysms of coughing. Returning to London, I left him in the hands of his carers and friends, like his ex-secretary Betty Richards and Mary Mclellan. He had insisted that I go out to spend time with my brother's family in Africa. It was some weeks later that we heard that his condition was giving cause for concern and a day later Mary took him to hospital again. Apparently he had left the house to transact some business and this had been too much for him. He lingered under morphine and saline drip for a couple of days. He died on 27th January 2000, Mother's birthday. She would have been ninety. He was ninety-five. His ashes joined with hers in the graveyard of Usk parish church.

Elaine had lived in retirement at Bexhill-on-Sea. The children and I had visited her in this home, which was but a stone's throw from the beach, on several occasions. Later as she became less able to look after herself she moved to Pilgrims Wood residential home in Guildford, Surrey. Elaine took the move philosophically and in her stride; it seemed a good place to spend her final years and she kept mentally alert almost to the end. At Homelawn House in Bexhill she had developed a passion for painting. She attended classes and exhibited at quite a high level. I still have a number of her paintings, mostly still life, decorating my living room. Elaine died aged ninety-one in 2002.

On the 9th June 2010 Elise phoned and told me that I had become a grandad of a girl, delivered the previous night. My granddaughter is called Amélie Chloe. At the time I was in the throes of a post-shingles depression and news of the new arrival certainly hastened my return to near normality. Since this time, Amélie has been six years of joy to me as she is a quick learner, forthright in her opinions and has a wide variety of interests. I am grandad "Bubbles" to her, which goes back to the times where she was a baby and loved the strings of bubbles I used to blow in her direction. She has enjoyed my reading to her from "Alice in Wonderland" with illustrations (by John Tenniel) taken from the original 1865 wood-blocks. Lewis Carroll, in his preface to the eighty-six thousand copies of the 1912 edition, one of which was obtained by my father when aged seventyish, is giving away the picture-book edition for the little ones at 1/- (shilling). The rest of the presumably adult readers paid 6/- (30p) each for their written illustrated editions, one of which was rescued from my father's library. Anyway, Amélie finds her princess books have recently replaced Alice in her affection and though americanised, they do include such well known British tales as Cinderella and Sleeping Beauty. Children today have a range of opportunities, so there is really no excuse for spending leisure hours in front of the computer or other screens. Amélie keeps Elise and Dom constantly on the move. Not only does she belong to Rainbows, rather akin to Cubs which I enjoyed, but she attends gymnastics, swimming and dance sessions which cost time and money. I enjoy seeing her progress in horse riding at the Trent Park stables in Cockfosters, a regular date for me on Sundays at present.

James's eldest boy, Hayden, has been diagnosed with autism. Physically he is like any other six year old, but mentally he lives in a different world. It is a world which is difficult for us to understand where contact by touch can take unusual forms. Texture, that is the surface character of an object, is of compelling importance, more so than the object's intrinsic self. This leads to prolonged activities like throwing grass in the air or picking flower heads, which are hard to understand. Some aspects of learning, like speech, are retarded, so a one to one tutorial educational framework is essential, preferably within the state system. Having tried to understand the condition through reading books and attending plays on the subject, I have enormous sympathy for Hayden and his carers, that is Clare and James, who have two other little boys also to consider. It takes great love, patience and understanding to manage their situation successfully.

Ellis, Hayden's younger brother, is nearly four and he has developed well since attending pre-school. James hopes, now he has a job which does not involve being on call at weekends, to enrol Ellis in football and karate classes. He is certainly no shrinking violet and this will channel his energies in a more constructive form perhaps. There had to be a Welsh connection somewhere in my family and that came with the naming of Dylan, born in December 2013. He arrived at 11.40pm in the North Middlesex hospital on the predicted day. He is a sturdy young man who is now speaking and beginning to make his opinions felt. Finally James and Clare's youngest, Kinley, arrived a year after Dylan, so will be two in December 2016. I didn't get to see him until two months after he was born as at his birth I was in Africa and then James' family went down with "flu". When we did meet I found him a bonny baby and he has remained so, easily the quietest and easiest to look after of all five grandchildren.

This brings me nearly to the end of this autobiography. Last week was my eightieth birthday. There was a surprise party of sixteen, mainly running friends organised by my coach and friend Alan Carter, at a restaurant in Enfield. I later found that photographer Colin Thurston had captured the entire occasion, including speeches, and put it out on Facebook. There I sit, a thorn between two roses, Amanda and Rachel, with Wendy opposite. It was a lovely evening, all the better for being a surprise. Thank you Alan and to all who came.

At University of the Third Age, one of my classes gave me a specially designed card picturing my favourite pastimes from gardening, to running, to history, to foreign travel and teaching. Kenya featured prominently and my own home family then met at the Enfield Toby Carvery the day after my eightieth for a family celebration dinner. Five grandchildren, son and daughter, and in-laws, enjoyed the carvery and beautiful gardens on another memorable occasion.

I know not what the future holds in store but I can reflect on a life full of interest, of fun and achievement which I hope I have been able to convey in the pages of my autobiography.

Acknowledgements

I should like to thank particularly Sylvia Coombs and Cliff Williams, members of Enfield University of the Third Age Autobiography group, who have encouraged and entertained me during the writing of this book. Sylvia and my brother Chris have both offered constructive criticism and advice which has been invaluable.

Sheila White, an accomplished artist from my home town of Potters Bar, created the cover design featuring the wheel of my life and Sophie Simpkin, also an artist, suggested the racy title. Walker McKone helped the book to reach a wider audience.

Lastly, I thank Prontaprint Potters Bar for printing the text and photographs; Vinay and James have shown great patience with my frequent interruptions. Also Richard Lee and Hardi Samsami, who were responsible for much of the printing in the first half of my book. Similarly my publisher Chella at Honeybee Books for giving me the chance to tell my story.

#0002 - 221117 - C12 - 210/148/10 - PB - 9781910616710